# THE
# INDOOR
# KITCHEN
# GARDEN

# THE
# INDOOR
# KITCHEN
# GARDEN

## VEGETABLE GROWING
## IN LIMITED SPACE

### JOY O. I. SPOCZYNSKA

*1817*

HARPER & ROW, PUBLISHERS, New York
Cambridge, Philadelphia, San Francisco, Washington
London, Mexico City, São Paulo, Singapore, Sydney

Designed and produced by
Breslich & Foss
Golden House
28-31 Great Pulteney Street
London W1R 3DD

Editor: Judy Martin
Designer: Roger Daniels
Illustrator: Nigel Hawtin

For information address Harper & Row, Publishers, Inc., 10 East 53rd Street,
New York, N.Y. 10022.
Published simultaneously in Canada by
Fitzhenry & Whiteside Limited.

Published in the United States of America by
Harper & Row, Publishers, Inc.
10 East 53rd Street
New York, New York 10022

FIRST U.S. EDITION

Library of Congress Cataloging-in-Publication Data
Spoczynska, Joy O. I.
        The Indoor Kitchen Garden.
        Includes index.
        1. Vegetable gardening. 2. Indoor gardening.
3. Container gardening. I. Title.
SB324.5.S66 1989    635′.048    88-45525
ISBN 0-06-016018-7

Printed and bound in Spain by Sirven Grafic
L. D. B-43-1989

# CONTENTS

# CONTAINER VEGETABLE GARDENING

Indoor gardening has become an increasingly popular pastime during recent years, as many people who enjoy plants but have no outdoor garden area have realized the pleasure and simplicity of growing a wide range of ornamental houseplants. Plants producing edible fruits and vegetables have been rather neglected as candidates for container growing indoors, although a number are as attractive as they are useful. Although few outdoor gardeners have not at one time or another considered making over part of the garden to edible crops, it has been widely assumed that indoor conditions will not meet the requirements of most food plants.

This is not so, and from experience I can introduce you to simple cultivation methods for a wide range of vegetables and herbs that you can enjoy freshly harvested without the benefit of any outside growing area. If you have a patio or balcony where these plants can be sited, so much the better; it will save you space indoors. But if you do not have these facilities, it will make no difference to your gardening success.

## Where to start

Leaving aside for a moment the question of which vegetables you can or cannot grow in containers indoors, an important aspect of your choice of crops will be the amount of space in your home which you can allow for an indoor kitchen garden. Fortunately, the principle of this type of gardening does not disqualify one-room dwellers any more than the owners of large houses; restrictions on the area for the food crops mean only that you may wish to be more selective about what you grow in order to produce the most generous cropping within the available space.

Indoor gardening dispenses with the outdoor gardener's problems of local climate, changes in the weather, and the soil type in a given location. These conditions are within the control of the vegetable grower who works indoors. The single most important element in siting

**Growing under artificial light**
If you have a very limited space indoors with good enough light to grow food crops, you can give some of your plants a boost by providing an artificial light source. Daylight fluorescent tubes make extremely good growing lights and these can be fitted to shelving to provide a small extra growing area. Forty watt tubes fitted along the underside of a shelf shed a high light level on the shelf below which is beneficial to plant growth. The tubes do not generate as much heat as ordinary light bulbs, but you should make sure they are not immediately within range of the plant growth; a distance of 6in (15cm) or so from the top of the plants is adequate.

Herbs and small tomato plants are among the crops which do well under artificial light. However, to grow food plants permanently in an artificial light source requires an extended 'day length' and not all will thrive under such conditions; so fluorescent light is best considered as a useful supplement to sunlight rather than a substitute.

your plants must be to ensure that they obtain enough light not merely to grow but to thrive.

Sunlight is not just good for plants – it is actually life-giving. Plants manufacture their own food supplies by a process called photosynthesis, whereby the chlorophyll, or green coloring matter in the plant body, is converted into starches by the action of sunlight, which causes chemical changes. Many plants can continue to exist in light levels lower than those which they are naturally adapted to and prefer. But they cannot carry out all their functions if deprived of light, and this is especially important in food crops which are required to be productive as compared, say, to foliage houseplants which are expected to look decorative but do no more than that.

It follows, then, that your vegetable plants should be sited at or very close to a window to obtain the maximum amount of daylight. Light levels drop quite dramatically through the room as the distance from the window increases; it is not easy for us to appreciate these changes, as the light levels required for human sight are not comparable to those needed for healthy plant growth.

The ideal position for many of the plants is within a short distance of a window which receives full sun all day. Most will do very well in this situation but fortunately there are some which flourish easily in less direct sunlight. This means that you can make use of windows which receive sun only in the morning or evening, and even those on the side of the house facing away from the sun; simply choose the vegetables which can grow in that situation.

There is, of course, a notable exception to this rule in the case of mushrooms, a crop which obligingly utilizes dark corners in which to grow. Sprouting beans and seeds, a food source of great nutritional value, can also be sited in some convenient shady place. Germinating seeds do not need light, and filled seed trays can be placed out of sight under a bed, on shelves or on top of a high piece of furniture; they are then moved into the light when growth has appeared above the soil surface.

Even if you have only one well-lit windowsill where you can cultivate plants, you can obtain a useful crop of salad plants such as lettuce and tomatoes, a wonderful range of herbs or some of the smaller-growing vegetables such as French beans and sweet peppers. Using the process of small succession sowings (see page 18), you can start seeds in containers placed away from the window while a crop of plants further on in growth occupy the lightest position, eventually replacing the plants which have cropped with the next batch reaching maturity. This enables you to make economical use of space while arranging for a continuous supply of fresh produce.

## What to grow

A surprising number and variety of food crops can be successfully grown indoors, so it is not worth wasting effort on those which cannot develop efficiently in containers. Unsuitable vegetables include root crops such as beets and turnips, which need considerable depth below ground, and plants of the brassica family – such as cabbages and Brussels sprouts – which need a broad area above the soil. Cooking onions are also excluded from this method of cultivation, though you can grow salad onions plentifully in all seasons.

It is important not only to select the right types of vegetables, but also to select the varieties best suited to indoor growing. Not all garden vegetables will adapt to indoor conditions but new cultivars are being developed all the time, including dwarf plants which produce excellent crops but are intended for growing in restricted space.

The vegetables described individually in later chapters have been proved suitable for indoor cultivation through my own experience of growing them; the size and the flavor of each crop are all you would wish from fresh home-grown produce. I have recommended the named cultivars which I have found particularly successful. This is not to say these are the only types which you could grow indoors; cultivation of plants, like all things, has developed to some extent through trial and error. If you find these named cultivars are not available when you need them, study seed catalogues carefully to find varieties of comparable size and growing requirements. Seed suppliers often indicate plants suitable for containers and for indoor growing, and may be prepared to give advice as to the best choices. Some garden cultivars do prove adaptable, however, so it is worth experimenting with small sowings if you have enough space and the enthusiasm to risk a failure.

Having considered what you can grow, think carefully about what you want to grow. There is great fascination in watching a plant develop, flower and produce its fruit, and the less familiar varieties may represent a challenge, but do not be tempted to grow things that you will not eat. It is best to grow what you know you will use, in quantities that you can use while they are still fresh. Make a list of the vegetables that you cook with most frequently, and your preferences among the salad crops. Eliminate those which cannot be grown in the indoor garden and plan your container growing by reference to this list. Check container sizes and light requirements of the individual plants, so that you can estimate the area they will occupy.

Obtain a good selection of seed catalogues from reputable growers – you can find addresses in the advertisement sections of weekly or monthly gardening magazines – which provide descriptions and color photographs of the vegetables, as well as much useful advice on growing. Mail order service is usually highly efficient, so you can order your full range of seeds and will not have to wait long before you can start cultivation. If you have a well-stocked garden center locally, you will also find a number of the recommended varieties among the pre-packaged seeds on sale there.

## Choice of containers

Plants require not only light, water and nutrients, but also adequate space in the soil for their roots to spread out and anchor themselves. In most cases, the smaller pot sizes and shallow trays are not adequate to enable the root systems to develop in a way which supports the plant's growth above ground. Seeds can be started in small pots or seed trays, but as the seedlings develop into plants and the plants come to maturity, it is necessary to pot them on into larger containers. Advice is given in later chapters on pot sizes for individually potted plants and on spacing plants grown together in a large tub or trough, according to the type of vegetable grown. Arranging to provide sufficient surface area and depth of soil does not mean that your home will become crowded with huge, immovable tubs. A 7in (17cm) or 9in (23cm) pot size is in most cases the maximum container size to house a maturing plant.

You can use purpose-made plant pots in terracotta (clay) or plastic. Improvised or decorative containers may include wooden boxes and plastic or ceramic jugs and bowls. Avoid irregularly shaped containers which will not allow roots to radiate evenly from the plant base through the soil.

Good drainage is essential to the success of container-grown plants: in a warm indoor environment the growing medium in the pots may dry out quite quickly and the plants need regular and often frequent watering, but they certainly will not do well if allowed to become water-logged. If you are using containers which are not constructed with drainage holes, you will have to make provision. Punch or drill holes in wooden or plastic containers and stand them in trays which will collect the water that drains through the soil. If you are using more decorative pottery ware, put a layer of brick chippings, pebbles or coarse gravel in the bottom and either insert the growing medium on top of this or grow the plants in plastic pots placed inside the ceramic containers.

## What you need

Your stock of containers can be judged according to the space available for vegetable growing and the type of plants you intend to cultivate. Basic stock should include seed trays, which are available in small and large sizes, and 3in (8cm) pots for sowing and germinating the seeds, and a selection of pots up to the 9in (23cm) size for potting on growing plants in stages. Tubs and troughs are sometimes advisable for larger plants, or for easier handling of small group plantings, but are not always essential. Keep in mind that the larger containers are very heavy once filled with soil – even more so when they have been watered. Make sure that you will be able to move them if necessary and that they are well supported if standing above floor level.

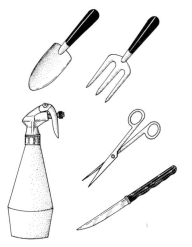

The indoor gardener does not need special gardening tools other than a small hand trowel and fork. As a dibber for making holes in the potting mixture to insert seedlings, a pencil is perfectly adequate. A small hand-held water spray is indispensable and you will find a sharp knife and a pair of scissors useful. You can improvise tools from old kitchen implements; spoons of all sizes are handy for topping up the soil in the containers and a soup ladle is invaluable for scooping growing medium out of its bag and into large pots with the minimum of mess.

Plastic propagators are available in various sizes for protection of germinating seeds and emerging seedlings; these basically consist of a seed tray fitted with a clear plastic cover. You can sow the seeds direct in the propagator tray, or stand smaller seed trays or pots inside it. Individual plastic propagator tops are also made to fit the standard pot sizes. If you are raising a number of crops, the outlay on these items can be

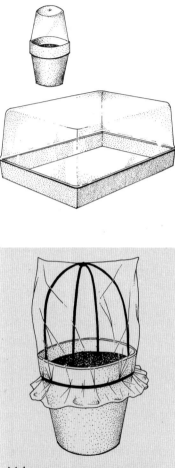

Make a propagator top to protect
germinating seeds and tiny
seedlings by inserting wire hoops
into the growing medium and
covering them with a clear plastic
bag secured below the pot rim.

quite expensive. An effective alternative is to put each pot in which
seed is sown into a clear plastic bag and seal it around the pot rim with a
strong rubber band. To create space above the soil, the bag can be
supported on two hoops of wire set at right angles to each other and
anchored by pressing them into the growing medium close to the sides
of the pot.

An electrically-heated propagator is certainly not essential, but if
you are interested in the more exotic vegetables and keen to start your
sowings early in the season, you may find it a useful investment.
Remember to take account of running costs as well as initial purchase
price when you are looking for a suitable model.

For supporting plants, you will need garden canes and garden twine
or soft string for tying in the plant stems. A quicker way of securing
plants is to use the plastic-covered wire closures supplied with plastic
bags for food and refuse. These are easily twisted into place and have the
advantage that they are more easily loosened if necessary as the plant
grows and can be re-used after the plants have finished cropping.

Plant labels are useful for identifying the type of seeds in the various
pots or the particular variety of vegetable you are growing. It is remark-
able how quickly you can forget what was sown in which container
when you are starting off several crops. Use an indelible marker pen or
pencil for writing on the labels, as the moisture in the atmosphere can
otherwise make the writing indistinct.

A good general fertilizer in liquid form is the final requirement. This
does improve the quality of the harvest (although I recommend using a
specially formulated feed for your tomato plants to get the finest
results). A liquid is the easiest type to use, as it can be added to the water
at regular intervals during your routine watering of the plants. Follow
the manufacturer's instructions accurately, as an overdose of fertilizer
can be damaging to a plant's roots.

# SOWING AND GROWING

This chapter explains the general principles of growing vegetables indoors. There are basic elements of sowing seed and cultivating the plants which are common to all types. To ensure the success of a particular crop, however, it is important to follow the details given in later chapters for each individual vegetable as the details of cultivation at each stage vary from plant to plant.

## Choice of seeds

The size of seed for the range of vegetables varies considerably; some are tiny and difficult to sow evenly, others quite large and easy to handle. If you buy an ordinary packet of seed, the quantity of seeds in the pack varies correspondingly, but for any type of plant, this is the most economical way of buying seed. You can alternatively use pelleted seeds; each seed is enclosed in an outer casing which disintegrates once it is sown into the damp soil. These are larger and more uniform in size, so it is possible to space them quite carefully and avoid wastage in thinning out the growing seedlings. However, because of their size there are fewer to a pack. They are more costly than ordinary seeds, so it is a matter of deciding whether you would rather have the convenience or the greater economy, depending on the size of crop you intend to raise and the number of seeds you may be able to use during one season.

To store seeds between sowings, leave the remainder in the packet and put this into an airtight screw-top jar, to prevent the seeds from being affected by moisture in the atmosphere. Store the jar in a cool place. Pelleted seeds keep for up to two years, but is is unwise to keep ordinary seeds for too long, as a relatively high percentage will not germinate successfully after a period of time. With the longer growing season for indoor vegetable gardening and the practice of succession sowing of small quantities, it should not be necessary to keep seed from one year to the next.

## The growing medium

For container gardening the growing medium needs to be free-draining but moisture-retentive, with a firm but open texture that allows the plants' roots to spread and find anchorage. If you have access to a supply of garden soil, this can be used as the basis of your own soil mixtures. Sieve it carefully to remove large clumps of earth and stones, and make sure it is free of weed roots and garden pests. You can obtain commercially produced bags of sedge peat, silver sand and humus, and also odour-free manure. These can be mixed into the soil in varying quantities to improve the texture and nutrient content.

It is simpler for the inexperienced gardener to buy large bags of good-quality potting mixture. There are several proprietary brands to choose from, and a reputable manufacturer will have ensured that the mixtures have balanced nutrient content and are free of soil-borne diseases and weed spores. Soil-based mixtures are also described as loam-based, loam being a type of good soil. The alternative is peat-based mixtures, also called soilless mixtures; these are generally more fibrous in texture and dry out more quickly than the soil-based types. Additional material such as sand and humus can be added to these commercially produced growing mediums to improve the drainage and moisture-retention as necessary.

You will find proprietary mixtures intended only for sowing and germinating seed. There are not formulated to supply the needs of a developing plant, so seedlings are then potted up into a slightly coarser and more nutritious growing medium, possibly through two or three grades until the plant is fully established. There is no advantage to using a sowing mixture for germinating vegetable seed and it is more efficient to select a good all-purpose growing medium at the start, which you can use for both sowing and potting on.

After harvesting your produce, the spent soil can be reused as the

### Recycling natural materials

*Humus*
In open ground, humus in the soil is made by the natural breakdown of plant materials. It provides enrichment which is valuable to the growth of plants. You can provide humus for container-grown plants using fallen leaves which can be gathered in woods and parks. Let the leaves dry out completely and crumble them to produce a fine texture which can be blended into the soil.

If you store leaves for making humus, do not keep them in plastic bags as they will retain moisture and develop mold. Dry the leaves and store them in paper bags or boxes.

*Lime*
You can buy garden lime in small and large quantities, but if you prefer to use a natural material which would otherwise be discarded, eggshells can be used to increase the lime content of your growing medium. Crush them very finely, as sharp fragments can cause damage to the most delicate roots in a plant's root system.

basis of a new soil mixture for new plantings. Turn out the pottings into a large plastic bag, remove any roots remaining in the soil and blend in some peat, humus and manure to improve the texture and replace lost nutrients.

## When to sow

Outdoors, the growth rate of seeds and plants is largely dependent on the weather conditions prevailing at any given stage in their development. Indoors, fluctuations in temperature can be kept to the minimum, watering and humidity are within your control; you do not have to face the extremes of drought, rainstorms, frost and snow. This enables you to sow earlier and enjoy earlier cropping, thus extending the growing season to a larger proportion of the year. There are also some vegetables which can be sown and grown almost throughout the year, including radishes, sprouting beans and mushrooms, so it is possible to obtain a continuous supply. Generally, however, for the majority of the crops the plant growth remains related to the seasons, in that seeds normally sown in spring outdoors are also started indoors in spring – but about four to six weeks earlier in the right conditions. You can continue harvesting crops well into autumn, as there is no fear of early frosts spoiling the vegetables.

## Succession sowing

To obtain the maximum amount of produce from your limited growing space you should practise the system of succession sowing, which provides usable amounts of vegetables continuously rather than a mass of plants all at the same time. Make small sowings at intervals of about two weeks, so that as one crop fully matures and is harvested, the next is just coming to the harvesting stage, and so on. Experience will soon tell you how many seeds to sow in one batch to meet your culinary requirements. You do need a good supply of containers to do this, from seed trays to large-size pots, as you will have several sowings in different stages at one time.

## Sowing the seeds

It is a common error to sow seeds too deeply in the soil. This delays the appearance of the seedlings above the soil surface after germination, and they have to waste energy in growing up towards the light which would be better spent in their development above ground. In the majority of cases, the seeds are sown just below the surface of the soil, about ¼in (5mm) deep; a few are sown at ½in (1cm) deep. There are one or two notable exceptions to this rule, such as broad beans and runner beans which are covered with 2in (5cm) depth of soil. Generally you can just scatter or place the seeds on the soil surface and cover them with a layer of potting mixture.

Saving your own seed for use in the next year's growing season is rarely practical. A proportion of the crops has to be allowed to run to seed – acceptable in a large garden which is densely planted, but a waste of cropping potential in container gardening. A number of the recommended varieties are F1 hybrids, which are unsuitable for self-seeding in any conditions.

To prepare the containers for sowing, fill them with potting mixture and firm the surface lightly. It should be level and smooth, but not heavily compacted. Moisten the soil before sowing and be sparing with the application of water; the soil should be damp to encourage germination, but not wet. If the underlying soil is damp there is no need to water again when you have covered the seeds. If the soil dries out before the new growth shows above the surface, it is better to dampen it with a spray rather than a watering can, as a jet of water can disturb the germinating seeds which are just beginning to root in the soil.

Young plants need space to develop from the earliest stages, so there is no advantage to letting the seeds lie thickly in the soil. If you need a large crop, use more containers with fewer seeds in each. If the seeds are too small to be placed separately at suitably spaced distances from each other, sow them very thinly to save wastage and make it easier to thin out the seedlings as they grow. When the seeds are in place, simply sprinkle a top layer of potting mixture over them to the required depth.

## Germination

Germinating seeds need warmth and moisture, but light is not essential. In fact, most should germinate in the dark, and a shady location will do no harm to those which can germinate in light. You can place the containers in a closet, or in a utility room or basement with no windows, provided that the temperature is high enough and evenly maintained. If the seed trays or pots must stand in the light, a simple solution is to cover them with a sheet of black plastic. You can cut pieces from an opaque plastic refuse bag and place them over the containers; there is no need to tie them on as this prevents ventilation.

The even warmth of central heating provides ideal conditions for germinating seeds, but it may have a drying effect so it is necessary to monitor the moisture content of the soil. If your home does not have central heating, keep the containers in the warmest place least exposed to currents of air and sudden temperature changes. Do not site them close to a gas fire or cooker, as the fumes are detrimental.

As soon as the seedlings show above the soil surface, remove the coverings and place the containers in the light.

## Transplanting and potting on

As the seedlings develop and the growth begins to spread, they should be moved on to larger containers. One plant per pot is the ideal, but if

Seedlings can be moved to a larger container when they have developed a few true leaves in addition to the cotyledons, the small pair of seed leaves which are first to appear.

Use an ordinary kitchen fork to support and lift a seedling when it is being transferred from one pot to another.

you are short of space, three or four seedlings can be transplanted into a larger pot and may be potted on again at a later stage if the container is not large enough to support them all. Remember that the point of using larger containers is not only to provide room for the top growth, but also for the roots which are establishing within the soil. It is often more important that the plants are given greater soil depth as they grow, rather than space to spread laterally.

The first pair of leaves which appear after germination are the cotyledons, or seed leaves, which contain the young plant's food supply. The first transplanting should be made when the seedlings have developed at least two or more true leaves after the appearance of the cotyledons. Prepare the new container before you lift the seedlings, firming in the potting mixture and making a hole in the soil to receive the tiny plant. It can be difficult to grip the fine stem of a seedling without causing damage. A kitchen fork is a useful implement for transplanting: slip two tines of the fork around the main stem of the plant just below the cotyledons, and use the fork to lift the seedling gently. You may need to loosen the soil carefully to work the seedling free; a plant label is useful for this task, but be careful not to cut through delicate roots when you disturb the potting mixture.

Lower the seedling into the new container and lightly press the soil around the roots and plant base to anchor it well in position. Water the soil very moderately with tepid water, carefully applied to avoid wetting the plant. Place the containers in a light position, but do not put seedlings in full sun where they will be scorched. If the plants are on a brightly lit windowsill, put newspaper between the container and window pane to shade the seedlings during times of day when the sun is strongest.

Unless you have been able to move the seedlings directly into their final containers, they should be potted on again when four or more leaves have developed around the central growing point. Continual repotting is not encouraging to the plants' growth, and root disturbance is usually resented at any stage. If the plants seem a little sluggish after transfer to a new container, leave them time to re-establish and resume growth. Do not supply extra water or fertilizer in the hope of reviving them; this runs the risk of doing more damage through over-watering and scorching of the roots.

## Supporting plants

Low-growing vegetables or those which do not produce branching growth present no problems in container growing. The larger varieties can become quite heavy, the more so as the fruits set and develop towards harvest. Tomatoes, cucumbers, beans and peas are among the plants which require some form of support from quite an early stage. Cucumbers are also among those plants which actually produce a better crop if well-supported.

A tomato plant is adequately supported when tied in to a single sturdy cane. Melons require a construction of canes and wire which trains the lateral shoots horizontally, and the heavy fruits need the support of nets. The method of support for each vegetable is explained under the relevant heading.

## Pollination

Sex is essential even in the vegetable garden. If the seeds are not pollinated – fertilized by the pollen of the male flowers – then there will be no development of fruits, and a number of the vegetables which you may wish to grow are technically the fruits of the plant. There is a general exception to this rule in the case of all-female hybrid plants, which do not require pollination. Several of the recommended cultivars are of this type and you should keep a note when you are ordering seeds

Most of the larger-growing vegetable plants require some form of support; a single cane is adequate for main stems, but certain plants need a more complex framework.

22

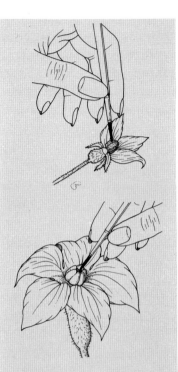

**Pollination**
Use a fine camel-hair brush to transfer pollen from the ripe anthers of the fully developed male flower on to the stigma of a fully open female flower. This is all that is involved in hand-pollination, although you can, if you wish, lightly spray the plant with tepid water after pollinating, especially in dry conditions; but avoid spraying the stigmas of the female flowers, as this will wash off the transferred pollen.

as to the category of the plant for reference when the time comes for pollination.

If your plants are growing outside on a patio, rooftop or balcony when they come into flower, all well and good: the bees will find them and they will be pollinated naturally. But in the indoor kitchen garden, you will have to do the bees' job for them, fertilizing the plants by hand-pollination.

Pollination is essential to the productivity of melons, eggplants, zucchinis and other delicacies. You will need to study the flowers to identify the male and female parts. In the large flowers of the zucchini, for example, these are easy to see. The male flower is dissected down the middle; the anthers are the male sexual parts which contain the pollen grains. In the female, there is a swelling at the base of the flower (the future zucchini) containing the ovules, or unripe seeds.

On pollination, during which the fine, dust-like pollen is deposited on the stigma (the sticky top of the style in the female flower) each pollen grain sends a microscopic tube down into the ovary, travelling down inside the style until it reaches one of the ovules. The tube penetrates the ovule and fertilizes it; this, when it ripens, becomes the seed. This is sexual reproduction, as distinct from propagation of plants, and this brief biology lesson helps to explain what it is you are doing when you hand-pollinate a plant.

The method illustrated here is a general guide which should ensure good results. In a few cases I recommend a different pollination method – for tomato plants, for example – when the flowers are small and difficult to handle. The alternative process is simply to spray the plants well on several successive days once the flowers have begun to open. This serves to disperse the pollen and the repeated sprayings take account of the fact that the flower buds on a single plant will be opening over a period rather than all at once.

There are a few cases in which male flowers on the same plant as the female should not be allowed to pollinate it; in this case, you just remove the male flowers to make sure that the pollen which reaches the stigma has come from a male flower of another plant, or hand-pollinate from plant to plant.

## Pests and diseases

The relative lack of trouble from plant diseases and pests is another advantage of indoor growing but cannot be discounted altogether, especially during fine weather when you may wish to keep windows and doors open or stand the containers outdoors. Slugs and snails enjoy leafy growth of all kinds and may be found under the rim or on the soil of containers placed outside; they also from time to time come indoors through an open window. These are easily seen, however, and removed. If you bring containers back inside from an outdoor position, check that you have no unwelcome visitors.

Bean crops are susceptible to blackfly, though I have never found this a problem with indoor gardening. Should you discover these tiny black aphids infesting your plants, you can remove them effectively without resort to chemical pesticides. Use ordinary soap and water to create a good lather and spray the foam forcefully on to the affected stems and on leaves. The blackfly will not survive this treatment, but it will do no damage to the plants.

Eggplants are commonly troubled by red spider mite. Fortunately, these too are less likely to attack container-grown plants, but if they do, they can be defeated by nothing more lethal than tepid water. Spray generously until the pests disappear; this treatment is also good for the plant, which needs a warm, moist atmosphere.

# THE INDOOR HERB GARDEN

**Stem cuttings**
All of the vegetables described in this book are propagated from seed, but with herbs such as rosemary, mint and sage, new plants can be grown from stem cuttings taken from established specimens. Select a healthy shoot with a vigorous growing tip and cut the stem at an angle below a leaf joint. Strip away the lower leaves and insert the stem in a small pot filled with a sandy potting mixture. Water lightly and place the pot on a windowsill, in gentle warmth but shielded from direct sun, until new top growth indicates that the cutting has rooted. Transfer it to a larger pot size as the developing plant outgrows its original container.

**H**erbs are among the most rewarding of food crops for indoor growing. They produce results quickly and besides adding their aromatic and distinctive flavor to hot and cold dishes of all kinds, they make an attractive display growing in pots on a sunny windowsill. There are some herbs, both popular and unusual varieties, which are not suited to container-growing indoors, because they need a steady high temperature or plenty of root space to develop useful growth; but there is an excellent range of widely enjoyed herbs which can be readily propagated and grown under indoor conditions.

The indoor growing conditions for herbs are much the same as those generally required for most houseplants; a reasonably even temperature in a well-lit, fairly humid location, with protection from extremes such as fierce direct sun or low night-time temperatures. The right environment is easy to attain during summer months, but some herbs can be grown through the winter to provide fresh, leafy growth, and will need a little more care when indoor and outdoor temperatures are highly contrasted – they should be grown at or very close to a window to take advantage of all available light, but should not be exposed to cold currents of air or allowed to stand with their leaves pressed against frosted window panes.

## Cultivation of herbs

Most of the herbs recommended here can grow well in small to medium-sized pots so need not take up much space; alternatively you can plant them together in a trough or box. They look pretty in earthenware containers, including parsley and strawberry pots which have holes in the pot sides through which the plants can grow as well as the wider opening at the neck of the pot. A few need a good depth of soil for adequate root development, while others thrive in confinement; the best conditions are described for each individual herb. Container growing tends to restrict plant growth, so the herb plants do not attain the height and spread that they would achieve in the open garden. But this can be a positive advantage, as in the case of mint, which in the open garden rapidly spreads across all the available space, and with the bushy or shrubby types, such as thyme, rosemary and bay, which can be clipped and controlled to encourage a compact shape and fresh new growth.

Good drainage is essential, as too much moisture at the roots is inevitably damaging. Make sure that the potting medium is free-draining; you can stand the containers on a tray of pebbles so that the moisture escaping from the bottom of the pots contributes to a moist atmosphere around the growing plants. Provide a good-quality soil-based growing medium: container-grown herbs rapidly extract the nutrients from the soil and may benefit from occasional feeding during the period of full growth.

## Using herbs in the kitchen

The main purpose and advantage of growing herbs indoors is of course to have fresh leaves immediately to hand for flavoring cooked dishes and salads. (If you keep the herb pots in the kitchen, make sure they are out of range of gas fumes, concentrations of steam and the radical changes of temperature caused by cooking appliances.) Salads, sandwiches, snack foods, roast meats, casseroles and stews, and vegetarian dishes all benefit from the true taste of fresh herbs. But if your crops do well, you may also wish to store some of the produce, and the leaves can alternatively be dried or stored in the freezer.

Leaves for drying should be spread on an absorbent surface, not on wire racks; a piece of muslin stretched over a wooden frame makes an ideal drying rack for herbs. Allow them to dry in warm, airy conditions, but not in direct sun, to maintain color and flavor. Dry whole sprigs of the herbs and strip leaves from stems after they are dry. Store the leaves in airtight containers, to prevent reabsorption of moisture, where they will keep for six to eight months.

You can freeze whole leaves or leafy stems, storing them in plastic bags or tubs. Chives are better when chopped before freezing, and it is convenient to keep a supply of chopped parsley, too, as this is a herb with endless culinary uses.

# Basil

*Ocimum basilicum*
Annual

The lush green leaves of sweet basil provide a strong and distinctive flavor much appreciated for a wide range of culinary uses. In its native conditions it is a perennial plant which can grow up to 3ft (90cm) high, but for container cultivation should be grown as an annual and will not achieve full height. A dwarf form (*O. minimum*) is available particularly suited to indoor growing; this has slightly smaller leaves and a more delicate flavor.

### Cultivation

Sow in early spring, two or three seeds to a half-pot containing a good soil-based growing medium. Maintain a minimum temperature of 55°F (13°C) during germination. As the seedlings develop, pot on into larger containers; up to six plants of the smaller variety can be grown to maturity in an 8in (20cm) pot. Water freely and pinch out flower shoots as they develop. Harvest the leaves from mid to late summer onwards.

### Culinary uses

Basil is recognized as the perfect accompaniment for tomatoes, raw and cooked, and is in fact an excellent flavouring for a wide range of vegetables. It can be added to meat, fish and poultry cooked in a variety of ways, and is excellent in egg and cheese dishes. Sauces benefit from the addition of chopped basil; the flavour of this herb is enhanced rather than diminished when it is cooked. It is the main ingredient of the delicious pesto sauce for pasta.

# Bay

*Laurus nobilis*
Evergreen shrub

In open ground the aromatic bay can attain tree-like growth, but kept in a large tub can be trimmed to maintain a compact, attractive shape which provides flavourful leaves all year round.

## Cultivation

Obtain a young plant and grow on in good-quality soil-based potting medium. Provide a warm, sunny location. Pot on as necessary until the shrub can be maintained permanently in a large tub, keeping the growth trimmed to control size. Bay can be propagated by stem cuttings taken in summer and rooted in sandy soil. Take leaves at any time of year for use fresh or dried.

## Culinary uses

Bay is an ingredient of bouquet garni, along with parsley, thyme and marjoram. It provides subtle flavouring for casserole dishes, stews and roasted meats, fish and fish stock; remove the bay leaves at the serving stage or before eating. It may be added to marinades, and imparts a delicate flavor if infused in milk to be used for making sauces.

# Chervil

*Anthriscus cerefolium*
Biennial

Chervil is an attractive herb, with its feathery foliage and summer flowers; growth reaches between 12in (30cm) and 20in (50cm) in height. The delicate, sweet taste can be added to your cooking through winter as well as summer, by means of repeated small sowings which yield a harvest in under two months.

## Cultivation

Chervil can be grown as a biennial to supply two crops from one sowing, the first within six to nine weeks of sowing and another before the flowers appear in the second year of growth. Alternatively, it can be grown as an annual and the plants discarded when the best leaves have been taken.

Sow in pots and trays in small quantities; transplant to larger pots or troughs as growth develops, and provide a rich, moist but free-draining soil. Place in good light or partial shade, but do not expose the plants to direct sun, which encourages them to run to seed.

Arrange succession sowings from early spring for summer crops; from late summer to early autumn for winter use. Take the outer leaves when harvesting, leaving the center of the plant to produce new growth. Chervil should be picked immediately before use.

## Culinary uses

This is a mild-flavored herb which may be used as an ingedient or a garnish. Use it to make herb butter for fish and poultry or add it to the final cooking stage of soups and sauces. It enhances the flavor of other herbs when they are used in combination. It is particularly good in omelettes and other egg dishes and chopped chervil makes a pleasant garnish for roast meats and vegetables.

# Chives

*Allium schoenoprasum*
Perennial

The long tubular leaves of chives grow in grass-like clumps 10-12in (25-30cm) high and it is these, not the fine onion-like white bulbs, which are the edible part of the plant. Attractive purple flowers are borne on tall straight stems above the foliage and as the plant does not need full sun all the time to grow well, it makes an attractive feature on any brightly lit windowsill.

## Cultivation

Sow in early spring and pot on the young plants when large enough to handle to 6in (15cm) apart; chives grow well in a trough or large pot as they need a reasonable amount of root space. Provide a light, soil-based growing medium and water generously. Cut the leaves from close to the base of the plant during summer.

Alternatively, you can start your stock from a bought pot-grown specimen, or ask a gardener friend for a divided section from an existing clump.

## Culinary uses

Use chives fresh, or chop them for freezing; they are not suitable for drying. The mild onion flavor is an excellent addition to sour cream and yogurt dressings, sandwich fillings, cream and cottage cheeses and fresh salad vegetables. Chives are particularly good sprinkled over hot potatoes or cold potato salads, but this is one of the most versatile herbs which can be used quite freely.

---

# Dill

*Anethum graveolens*
Annual

This is a plant that can grow to 3ft (90cm) tall, though it will usually achieve less height when pot-grown. The feathery green leaves are as attractive as they are aromatic and the seeds produced by the large flowerheads are also useful for cooking.

## Cultivation

Dill is relatively easy to grow, unfussy about the type of soil as long as it is well drained. Sow seeds in a large pot in spring and allow them to germinate in the dark; this takes about 14 days. Move the emerging plants to a sunny position. Pot on into larger containers if necessary; dill is quite a large plant which needs good root space. Harvest the leaves

when the plant is about 12in (30cm) high. Pruning controls the spread of the mature plant, and the prunings are not wasted as they can be used for cooking.

For a long growing season, sow successively during spring and early summer.

## Culinary uses

Dill is particularly associated with fish dishes, and also goes well with lamb and chicken. It is a good addition to sauces, mayonnaises and salad dressings. The seeds can be used as well as the leaves; these are harvested as they turn brown, dried on the seedheads and shaken loose. Dill seed is an important ingredient of pickles and can be used in baking sweet pies and cakes.

# Garlic

*Allium sativum*
Annual

The powerful flavor and odor of garlic make it very much a matter of personal taste. Devotees will use it raw and cooked in a wide range of dishes, so it is useful to know that new bulbs can be easily grown from garlic cloves. The plants grow to 12in (30cm) or more high, but it is what remains below the soil that is of interest.

## Cultivation

Separate the cloves in a garlic bulb and discard the smallest. Plant a single clove to a small pot in a rich, fertile growing medium. Stand the pots in a sunny location. Pot on the growing plants as necessary to allow space for the bulb to develop. The bulb is lifted when the leaves of the plant begin to die down; it may take about 6 months to obtain a harvest; for example, from early spring planting to autumn lifting. Hang the bulb to dry in a lightly-shaded, airy position, and discard leaves and stems to use the cloves only.

### Culinary uses

Some people never develop a taste for garlic; others feel no recipe is complete without it. Commonly used crushed or finely chopped, garlic provides piquant flavoring for foods of all kinds – soups, sauces, stews; meats, vegetables and pulses. For salads, it can be crushed or chopped into a dressing, or the salad bowl can be rubbed with a garlic clove before the fresh vegetables are put in, to impart a mild garlic flavor.

# Marjoram

*Origanum vulgare*
Perennial

There are many different types of marjoram; wild marjoram is a sweetly scented bushy plant; sweet marjoram (*O. majorana*) similarly produces bushy growth, and both of these plants grow to 8-10in (20-25cm) in height. Pot marjoram (*O. onites*) is a lower-growing type, producing small mounds of foliage about 6in (15cm) high, and its fragrance is slightly less than that of the larger types.

### Cultivation

Sow seed in early spring for summer cropping and maintain a warm, humid atmosphere; marjoram takes from two to four weeks to germinate and can be difficult to grow from seed. Pot on individually into 5in (13cm) pots or transplant into troughs at 9in (23cm) apart. A sunny position is essential. Remove flower buds as they appear to encourage new foliage growth.

Alternatively, obtain stem cuttings or rooted clumps from existing plants and pot them up in a light soil-based potting medium.

### Culinary uses

Marjoram is a particularly sympathetic herb for use in nut, bean and pasta dishes, but more traditionally is associated with roast meats, poultry and game. It is a useful ingredient of sausage meats and stuffings.

33

# Mint

*Mentha spicata*
Perennial

The mint commonly grown for culinary use is spearmint with its cool, fresh flavor, but as mint is easy to grow you may like to try some of the many other varieties, including peppermint, applemint and pineapple mint. Mint is an erect plant growing 12-18in (30-45cm) high. In the garden, the main problem is to stop it spreading out of control, so container growing is ideal as it necessarily confines the root spread; however, the roots do need a large, deep pot and growth will be too restricted if there is not enough depth as well as surface area of soil.

## Cultivation

Start your stock of mint in early spring from a stem cutting, rooted runner or small pot-grown plant. Plant up in a 9in (23cm) pot in a rich growing medium. Keep it out of direct sun and water generously, but make sure the roots do not become waterlogged. Mint thrives even when neglected, so the initial planting should quickly spread and fill the pot. You can then take cuttings from your own stock and bring them on in the same way. Pinch out flowerheads, as these are of no value and only distract the plant from leaf production.

## Culinary uses

Mint is another good kitchen standby, a fresh, sweet flavor complementary to many foods, fresh and cooked. Root and green vegetables benefit from a sprig of mint added to the cooking water, or chopped mint sprinkled on as a garnish before serving. It adds a light, clean taste to salads and dressings. Among meats, it is traditionally associated with lamb, as a cooking ingredient or made into a sauce or jelly to be served with roast lamb. It is a valuable herb for sweet dishes and cooling drinks; add it to desserts and cakes, fruit salad and fresh fruit drinks. Mint leaves can be frozen into ice cubes for summer beverages, to release their flavor slowly and subtly.

# Parsley

*Petroselinum crispum*
Biennial

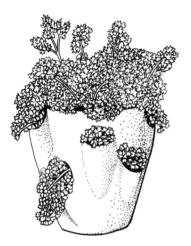

The best parsley growth occurs in the first year, and although it is biennial it is commonly grown as an annual. The fresh taste is complementary to dishes of all types, as an ingredient or as garnish. It is not the easiest of herbs to grow and is extremely slow to germinate, but because it is so versatile it is worthwhile having the patience to master the art of cultivating parsley. The plants grow between 8in (20cm) and 12in (30cm) high and make an attractive display.

## Cultivation

Sow in a rich, free-draining potting medium in pots or seed trays. Provide a warm and humid atmosphere and supply moisture to the soil during the germination period, which can be as long as eight weeks. As the seedlings appear, move the container to full light and thin out the planting. Parsley plants can be potted on into individual containers – a 4in (10cm) pot is adequate – but must be treated carefully as root disturbance is resented. They look particularly pretty when grown together in a ceramic parsley pot. For a continuous supply, carry out succession sowings from early spring through summer.

Because of the slow germination period, containers of parsley seeds take up space unproductively for some time. If you prefer to take a short cut, buy pot-grown plants or obtain rooted stems from the vegetable market or from gardening friends. Plant them up in individual pots or well-spaced in a large container.

## Culinary uses

Parsley must be the universal herb, as an ingredient and a garnish. It is a valuable food rich in vitamins. The fresh taste is indescribable, but quite distinctive. Mix it into dishes based on rice, beans, pulses or mixed vegetables, add it to soups, stews or sauces, meats, poultry and fish dishes.

# Rosemary

*Rosmarinus officinalis*
Perennial

Rosemary is a shrubby plant with needle-like leaves which can grow up to 5ft (1.5m) high. With careful pruning it can be maintained as a pot-grown indoor plant of a size up to about 2ft (60cm) and it makes an attractive sight when in flower. The flavor is strong in cooking and the growing plant is pleasantly aromatic.

## Cultivation

Sow in early spring in a light, sandy, soil-based potting mixture. Provide sufficient lime content by adding crushed eggshells or a small amount of garden lime. Transfer seedlings to small individual pots to grow on and keep them well watered. Seed-raised plants are not harvested until the second year. Water plants generously throughout their lives – the leaves quickly drop if conditions are to dry – but make sure the potting mixture drains freely as waterlogging will damage the roots.

Rosemary can also be propagated from cuttings taken during spring or early summer, or stock can be started from a purchased pot-grown plant. Do not be too quick to pot on a rosemary plant, as it tends to thrive when slightly pot-bound and gains no advantage from having a large area or depth of soil. Pruning not only controls the spread of this shrub, it helps to maintain vigorous, bushy growth.

## Culinary uses

Rosemary is another versatile cooking herb, suited to meat dishes or eggs and cheese. It makes a pleasantly aromatic contribution to broths, stews and risottos, and equally to marinades and vinegar dressings. It is particularly complementary to green vegetables and mushrooms.

The cosmetic value of rosemary has long been recognized in addition to its culinary uses. Water in which rosemary has been boiled makes an excellent skin freshener or a fragrant hair rinse for brunettes.

# Sage

*Salvia officinalis*
Perennial

The strongly fragrant, grey-green leaves of garden sage are associated with traditional recipes for roast meats and poultry, but there are many types of sage, including bushy plants up to 2ft (60cm) high and compact dwarf varieties. Golden and red-leaved varieties are decorative.

## Cultivation

It is not easy to grow sage from seed and as a single plant provides plenty of fresh foliage, the easiest way to start your supply is to buy a small pot-grown plant. Alternatively, take cuttings in spring from an established plant. Pot up the sage in light, free-draining soil and keep it in a sunny, warm location.

## Culinary uses

Sage has a strong flavor complementary to rich meats and is particularly associated with lamb and veal. It can be used in cooking roast meats and as an ingredient of stuffing mixtures. The taste also blends well with the stronger-tasting cheeses, and with cooked cheese.

# Tarragon

*Artemisia dracunculus sativa*
Perennial

There are two types of this herb and the best to grow is French tarragon (the other is called Russian tarragon) which has the stronger flavour for culinary use. It is a spreading, bushy plant up to 15in (38cm) high.

## Cultivation

Tarragon can be grown from seed sown in spring, but it is quicker to obtain a small pot-grown plant or to take cuttings which should be potted up in a light soil-based medium. As the plant increases in size, transfer it to a 5in (13cm) pot and trim the stems to keep the shape compact. Pot on as necessary up to a 9in (23cm) pot size. Pinch out flowering shoots as they appear.

## Culinary uses

Tarragon is a useful ingredient of sauces and dressing, notable as an essential ingredient of Sauce Tartare. In main dishes, it is highly complementary to chicken and turkey, fish and eggs.

# Thyme

*Thymus vulgaris*
Perennial

Thyme is an evergreen shrub growing 8-12in (20-30cm) high. The pleasantly aromatic leaves can be harvested at any time of year. Lemon thyme (*T. citriodorus*) is less powerful but the clean lemon taste is well suited to desserts, drinks and other sweet dishes.

## Cultivation

Sow seed in early spring and transplant seedlings into 3in (8cm) pots of rich, soil-based potting medium. Pot on to a larger pot size as necessary and site the pot in a place where the plant has a little room to spread. Prune back the growing tips to encourage branching and do not allow the plants to come into flower.

Thyme can also be propagated by cuttings or division of existing plants in spring. It is a good idea to divide established plants about every three years to maintain good growth. Discard old sections and pot up the healthiest divisions separately.

## Culinary uses

Thyme has a strong taste and should be used sparingly with other herbs, as it may overpower their contributions to the flavor of a dish. It is traditionally associated with roast meats and stuffings, but also goes very well with fish and shellfish. Add it also to pâtés and to vegetarian dishes based on pulses and nuts. Lemon thyme is especially suited to fish dishes.

# INDOOR SALAD CROPS

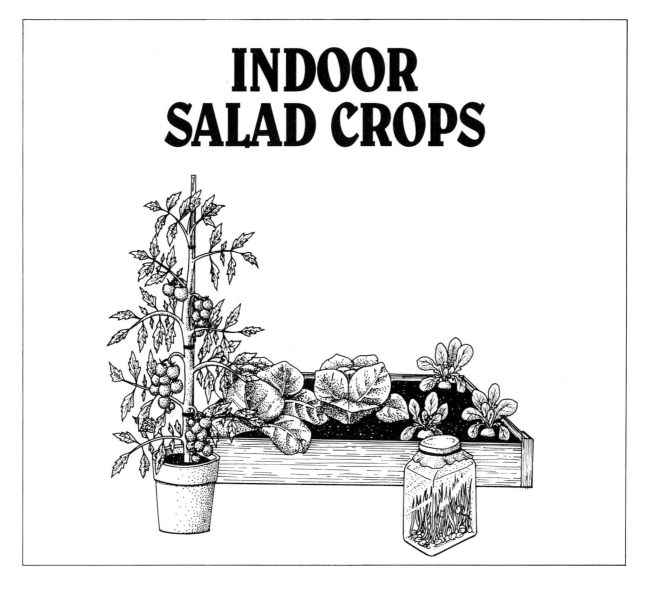

# CUCUMBERS

*Cucumbers are not the easiest of vegetables to grow, but if you choose the right varieties to start with and give them the regular care they need, you can produce a successful crop at your first attempt.*

As well as the usual salad uses, there are various recipes in which cucumbers can be included; they can even be stuffed and cooked. They are a more versatile vegetable than is sometimes appreciated, and are attractive plants to grow.

Cucumbers are divided into two main groups; greenhouse types and the outdoor varieties, also called 'ridge' cucumbers. The latter are not suitable for container-growing, requiring a large area and a lot of specialized attention and feeding. You should therefore confine your choice to the various greenhouse cultivars, which do not necessarily have to be grown in a greenhouse and can be successfully cultivated on a sunny windowsill indoors. The all-female hybrids need no pollinating and many of these types, although comparatively small and compact plants, produce cucumbers of adequate size for most culinary requirements.

## Cucumbers for indoor growing

The smallest cultivar, Fembaby, is an F1 hybrid often called the 'windowsill cucumber'. It has a curious history: one man spent eight years of his life breeding this hybrid in an effort to produce a cucumber small enough to provide supermarkets with whole cucumbers, rather than the halved large cucumbers commonly on sale. In fact, it turned out that customers preferred to buy the large cucumbers sliced in half: but horticulturists discovered that the new small variety was disease-resistant, cold-tolerant and compact in growth – ideal for growers without a greenhouse, who could grow it at home indoors at any window with a sunny aspect. Being an all-female hybrid, the plant does not need pollinating. In other words, it is a trouble-free cucumber for the indoor gardener, so Fembaby has now become a popular choice.

Fembaby produces the smallest cucumbers of any cultivar, averaging 8in (20cm). These are straight and well flavored. Other cultivars grow

---

### CULTIVATION CHECKLIST

Sow seed singly in 3in (8cm) pots and maintain 75°F (24°C) daytime temperature, 60°F (15°C) at night

Keep seedlings moist, fed and in good light

Pot on into 5in (12.5cm) pots after four true leaves have appeared

Transfer larger cultivars to 8in (20cm) pots for final development

Support stems with canes and pinch out growing points until fruits develop

Pick fruits as soon as ripe to encourage a second crop

into taller plants producing bigger cucumbers. I can recommend Telegraph Improved, an old favorite which has stood the test of time for indoor and outdoor growing. It is an all-round cultivar, a prolific cropper, and needs no pollination, but male flowers must be removed as they appear, as if they are allowed to pollinate the female flowers on the same plant, the cucumbers will be bitter.

Burpless Tasty Green F1 hybrid is a comparatively recent introduction, producing cucumbers 8-10in (20-25cm) long. This is an all-female hybrid which will not produce male flowers. A somewhat similar cultivar, but producing larger fruits, is Sweet Success F1 hybrid. The cucumbers are seedless and have a very sweet flavor. This strain is particularly disease-resistant and the cucumbers reach an average of 14in (35cm). It is also a faster-maturing variety; when sown in late spring, the plants can be fruiting within eight weeks of the young seedlings showing. Another prolific cropper is Conqueror, not a hybrid, so male flowers must be removed. These varieties are all equally at home indoors or out.

## Sowing and germination

All these cucumbers can be grown quite successfully in ordinary plant pots, a 5in (12.5cm) pot being quite big enough for growing Fembaby and an 8in (20cm) pot for the larger cultivars.

Spring is the best time to sow seed, but some cultivars may be sown at any time of year, provided that they have a sufficiently high initial temperature to ensure germination: 75°F (24°C) is not too high, and the night temperature must not drop below 60°F (15°C). If you can provide these conditions, winter sowings of cucumbers are a possibility; if not, wait until spring to start your crop.

My own method is to sow one seed per 3in (8cm) pot, the seed sown on edge ½in (1cm) deep. Cucumbers require a very rich and fertile soil.

Sow cucumber seed singly on edge in a 3in (8cm) pot.

**Indoor/outdoor growing**
Do not move cucumbers to an outdoor location until conditions are warm and sunny in late spring or early summer. They can be grown on a window ledge, balcony or patio provided the containers can be well-spaced to allow room for the plants to develop.

It is best to make your own potting medium, using one part loam, one part peat, one part humus, and one part well-rotted horse manure. The humus can be obtained by gathering dried leaves (see page 17) – oak, beech, sycamore, for example.

Failing this, use a commercial soil-based growing medium and mix in some humus, which you should be able to obtain from your garden center or usual supplier in bags of varying quantities. Use equal proportions of soil and humus to produce a rich, open-textured and free-draining potting mixture.

A little lime is beneficial, but do not overdo it – a small pinch per pot is sufficient. A sprinkling of bone meal will do no harm – a half-teaspoonful per pot is more than enough. Moisten the potting mixture before sowing with a fine spray of tepid water. While the seeds are germinating, stand the pots in saucers or trays so that they can be watered from below as necessary.

There is another method which indoor gardeners can use, which you may prefer to pot-growing. The containers used are large wooden boxes with a few holes punched in the bottom for drainage. A fertile bed is built up in layers – strawy manure about 6in (15cm) deep for the bottom layer; on top of this some turf placed upside down; and the rest of the box filled with finely sifted loam. The turf layer provides humus as the grass decays. This is a more demanding cultivation process, only suitable if you have plenty of space and want to produce a large crop.

## Growing on

As soon as the seedlings have appeared, move the pots to the lightest spot you can give them. A weak feed of very diluted fertilizer may be given fortnightly in these early stages. When the plants have produced four true leaves, after the initial appearance of the two seed leaves (cotyledons), transplant them to bigger pots – 5in (12.5cm) for all

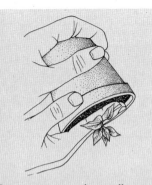

To remove a cucumber seedling from its pot, support the base of the plant between your fingers and turn the pot upside down. Tap the pot base to loosen the soil.

cultivars for the first re-potting and subsequently 8in (20cm) pots for all except Fembaby, which can stay in the smaller size.

Cucumbers are not the most resilient of plants, so when potting on you should use a method which causes minimum disturbance to the plants' roots. Rather than pulling or levering the plant from the soil, turn the pot upside down with your hand spread over the surface of the potting mixture, the stem of the plant loosely supported between your fingers. Tap the bottom of the pot to loosen the entire soil ball and handle it carefully in transferring the plant to the larger pot size, to avoid bruising or crushing the more delicate roots.

Do not neglect the routine of watering, spraying and occasional feeding. Given warmth and moisture, the plants will develop well towards the stage when they produce their flowers and can then be encouraged to set fruit. Remember to remove any male flowers which appear on non-female hybrid cultivars, or the cucumbers will become misshapen and bitter.

Pests should not prove troublesome. The main pest of cucumbers is the red spider mite, but it is more likely to attack greenhouse-grown plants than those grown in containers indoors. It is to be avoided, however, by spraying the plants regularly with tepid water. Mites hate moist conditions, but the cucumbers thrive in a damp atmosphere. Be sure to spray your plants every day if you have a drought.

## Supporting the plants

These small cucumber cultivars are climbers, and they need to be allowed to spread naturally if they are to produce a heavy crop. Maturing plants require support to encourage the final stages of development and to help them bear the weight of the ripening fruit. The main stem should be tied to an upright support, but laterals (side shoots) may be allowed to trail or cascade downwards, tied to separate supports if preferred. The laterals are often given the additional support of canes tied horizontally to the main vertical stakes.

The alternative common method of growing cucumbers is to support all stems upright (using thinner canes for the laterals than for the main stem), and to pinch out the growing points of the laterals at the second joint (above the second pair of leaves). Sub-laterals, the side shoots which grow in turn from the laterals, should be pinched out at the first joint. This treatment encourages the plant to produce fruits rather than additional leaves. Any large, unfruitful, leafy stems which may obscure the light from the flower-bearing stems should be removed.

## Harvesting

Spring-sown plants often produce fruit within seven or eight weeks, but some varieties take three to four months to develop the crop. Cut the cucumbers as soon as they are large enough; leaving them on the plants causes them to deteriorate quickly. The plants will usually produce further fruits after the first crop has been picked.

# SPROUTING BEANS AND SEEDS

*Sprouting is the simplest method of producing a food crop, and as well as the familiar mung beans used to produce delicious bean sprouts, there are other beans and seeds which quickly provide nutritious sprouted shoots useful for salads and cooked dishes.*

**B**ean sprouts are rich in vitamins and protein content. They contain iron and potassium, as well as fiber essential to good digestion. After four or five days, sprouted beans or seeds provide from six to eight times their original weight in nutritious elements, so they are a surprisingly valuable food source yet easy and quick to grow. In addition to mung beans, a vital ingredient of Chinese cooking, aduki and soya beans provide equally tasty, fresh sprouts within a short period.

Looking through a seed catalogue, you may come across names that you recognize without being quite sure how to grow the plants or use them in the kitchen. A number of seeds can be recommended for sprouting – alfalfa, fenugreek, triticale, and alphatoco, among the less well known items. Mustard and cress are more familiar examples which for little effort provide attractive greenery for sandwiches, salads and garnishes.

Do make sure when buying any kind of bean or seed for sprouting that it is labelled and recommended for human consumption. Similar products may be sold for field use or animal feedstuffs, and these are generally less expensive, especially if packaged in bulk; but they may have been subjected to chemical or other treatments which make them quite unsuitable for humans. Follow the advice given in growers' catalogues or on pre-packaged goods, and follow the rule that if in doubt, do not use unrecommended seeds to provide food.

### Mung beans

These green beans produce succulent shoots within a matter of days and provide you with fresh bean sprouts at any time of year. To sprout them you need a large glass jar, a piece of muslin or other porous cloth, and a rubber band.

Place a handful of beans in the bottom of the jar. Do not be tempted to put in too many, as the growing sprouts will need plenty of space to

---

**CULTIVATION CHECKLIST**

Place the beans or seeds in a glass jar; cover the top of the jar with muslin

— • —

Pour water through the muslin; rinse the beans or seeds and pour out the water; repeat twice

Place the jar in shade or darkness and carry out the rinsing procedure twice daily

— • —

Use the sprouts when they are about 2in (5cm) long and the mass is filling the jar

47

Mung beans

expand. Place the muslin over the top of the jar and secure it in place with the rubber band. Hold the jar under the cold tap and allow water to run through the top of the cloth into the jar. Swirl it around to rinse the beans thoroughly and pour the water out, again through the cloth. Repeat the rinsing twice more. Place the jar on its side in a suitable place where it can remain undisturbed. This does not have to be in complete darkness, although a shady position produces better results than a light one. In a warm location, the beans take less time to germinate than at ordinary room temperature.

Rinse the beans through twice a day, as described above, and after about three days in a fairly high temperature, or five days in a cooler location, you will see the husks split open and the tiny shoots appear. This is the advantage of using a glass jar as the container, as you can follow the progress of the bean shoots from the first sprouting to full development. After germination, the sprouts grow rapidly as you continue the twice-daily rinsing process. When they are 2in (5cm) or so long and filling the jar, they are ready for use. At this stage they are still growing, so if they are eaten immediately no nutrient value is lost.

Before putting the bean sprouts into a salad or using them for cooking, remove the husks. These usually rub off quite easily if the sprouts are rinsed under running water in a colander. Otherwise you can cut off the husks, but this wastes some of the nutrients.

Bean sprouts germinated in mid shade are pale green, but you can keep the jar in darkness to produce white shoots if preferred. The white shoots are good for cooking, while the green have an attractive appearance in a salad.

### Aduki beans

These beans are of Japanese origin and are advertised in many seed catalogues alongside the Chinese mung beans. They are sprouted in

Aduki beans

exactly the same way and can be used fresh or cooked in the same kinds of dishes. Their flavor is nuttier than that of the mung beans.

Soya beans

## Soya beans

It is quite difficult to grow soya bean plants to produce a bean crop, but it is easy to sprout them by the method described for mung and aduki beans. The advantage of soya beans is that they germinate more quickly, and germination can be accelerated even more by soaking the beans in tepid water overnight before starting the twice-daily rinsing procedure.

Alfalfa

## Alfalfa

Alfalfa, sometimes called lucerne, has been used for a long time as animal fodder and green manure, but has only quite recently come into use as an edible product for human consumption. It can be grown as a plant or sprouted and used in the same way as bean sprouts.

To sprout alfalfa, put a handful in a glass jar just as for the sprouting beans, and carry out the rinsing process. The only difference is that a higher temperature is needed to ensure germination – 68-70°F (18-20°C). The sprouts will be ready to eat five days after starting.

You can also grow alfalfa as an alternative to mustard and cress by sowing the seed on moist tissues or kitchen paper towels placed in a shallow dish. The crop is ready for cutting in five days and produces several harvests from one sowing, at about five-day intervals. The shoots stay in good condition in the salad compartment of a refrigerator for up to four days, but are not suitable for freezing.

Fenugreek

## Fenugreek

The seeds of fenugreek germinate rapidly and the fresh young sprouts have a flavor reminiscent of curry, which becomes milder as the

Triticale

Alphatoco

Mustard and cress

sprouts mature. You can harvest them early to take advantage of the spicy flavor. Fenugreek sprouts are rich in protein, iron and vitamin A. You can eat them raw in salads or add them to casseroles and stews.

### Triticale

These seeds are excellent for sprouting, germinated by the method described above. They are said to keep better than other bean or seed shoots, and will last for about 14 days if stored in a sealed plastic bag in the refrigerator. This is a useful quality, but it should be remembered that all sprouts are at their best for eating when freshly cropped. Triticale sprouts are excellent for salads and stir-fried dishes, or may be lightly steamed in a colander over a saucepan of boiling water.

### Alphatoco

This is a fairly recent introduction to the sprouting-seed market. These are grown as for the other types, but offer a sweeter flavor than any of those listed above. They can be used in the same way as triticale sprouts.

### Mustard and cress

An old favorite among sprouting seeds, and one which has introduced generations of children to the joys of growing edible crops, mustard and cress are easy to grow and will provide two or more harvests from one sowing. The seeds can be sprouted on any permanently moist substratum – blotting paper was the traditional favourite, but these days kitchen paper towels or tissues are the most convenient materials.

Place the damp tissues flat in a shallow dish and sprinkle on the seed. Sow the mustard three days later than the cress for both crops to mature at the same time. Once the seed is sown, you need only remember to keep the base layer moist at all times. Keep the dish shaded at first and move it to the light as the shoots appear.

# GREEN ONIONS

Green onions are also known as spring
onions, but indoors can be grown
throughout the year to provide tasty
flavoring for salads and cooked dishes.

**S**alads, of course, are not the only destiny of these small onions. You can use them chopped as an alternative to chives in omelettes and cheese dishes and the green parts also make a tasty garnish which you may like to use in place of parsley and other herbs, a useful variation particularly good for meat dishes. While young and slender, green onions are mildly flavored; as they mature and the stems thicken at the base, the taste acquires more 'bite'. The white bulbous tip is excellent sliced into salad to add piquancy.

Large-bulb cooking onions are not suitable for container gardening, as they need the space of the open garden to develop their bulb and root systems. If you want onion-flavored seasoning for raw vegetables, cheeses and cooked dishes, it is worth cultivating a large pot of chives (see page 30) in addition to your green onions. You could also try growing the silver-skinned varieties of small 'button' onions for pickling.

### Selecting green onions for indoor growing

The best variety to grow is White Lisbon, an established favorite. A newer type is Ishikura, which is a straight-growing form from tip to root, with no bulbous base. Green onions are specially bred for the salad bowl and however cultivated do not develop the large bulbs suitable for cooking.

### Sowing and growing

To ensure a continuous supply of green onions, sow seed at fortnightly intervals from early spring onwards. Salad onions are not fussy about the kind of soil. Your usual potting medium is perfectly adequate. Sow the seeds as thinly as possible – which is difficult as the seeds are very small – and be prepared to thin out the seedlings as they grow. Use deep containers such as pots and troughs – a shallow tray does not give

---

**CULTIVATION CHECKLIST**

Sow seed thinly and keep warm and moist to encourage germination

— • —

Thin gradually until plants are 3in (8cm) apart

— • —

Continue watering; provide an occasional liquid feed

— • —

Harvest when stems are thickened to the required size; pull young plants for mild flavor, grow on to develop thicker stems and stronger taste

**Indoor/outdoor growing**
Make small succession sowings of green onions in troughs or window boxes outdoors from late spring through summer. Indoor-sown plants can be placed outside at any time provided there is no danger of frost.

enough room for the root systems to develop. Germination takes between two and three weeks.

As the plants develop, water freely and do not allow the soil to dry out; but be careful not to go to the other extreme and allow the containers to become waterlogged, as this will cause the plants' roots to rot.

If you want the onions to develop strongly and grow thick stems with a good strong flavor, thin the plants out to 3in (8cm) apart. If the containers are large enough to allow more than one row of plants, see that these are not less than 6in (15cm) apart. You can carry out the thinning gradually, to reduce the amount of wastage from your original sowing. Make the use of the young plants in your cooking as they are pulled, removing them gradually until the remaining plants are evenly spaced. The thinnings provide mild green onions as the crop develops, and those left to thicken and grow larger will contribute a stronger taste to salads and cooked dishes. Encourage strong growth with an occasional liquid feed.

Seed sown in late summer and early autumn will keep you provided with salad onions right through the winter. You will obtain the main harvest from about two months after sowing. Site the containers on a well-lit windowsill to take advantage of all the available light during short winter days.

# TOMATOES

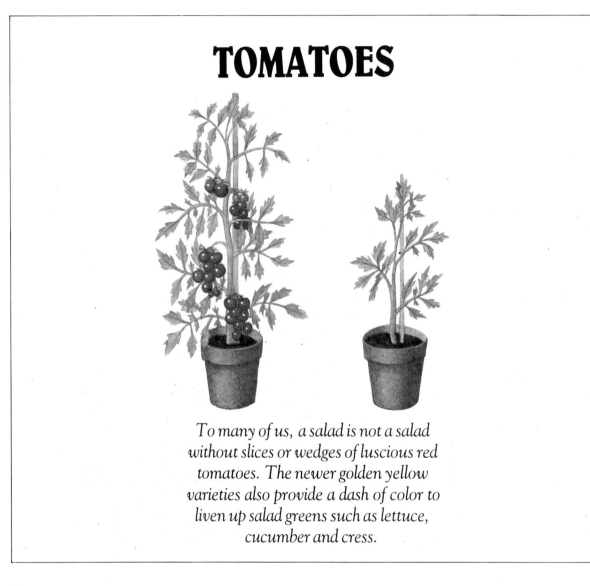

*To many of us, a salad is not a salad
without slices or wedges of luscious red
tomatoes. The newer golden yellow
varieties also provide a dash of color to
liven up salad greens such as lettuce,
cucumber and cress.*

omatoes are rewarding indoor plants, as I can testify from a huge crop harvested one year from only three sunny windowsills in my apartment. They are quite decorative while in flower and fruit, besides providing a continuous supply of one of the most tasty and versatile vegetables. The pleasure of eating firm, sweet salad tomatoes is easily matched by the many and various recipes for cooking them as a side vegetable and an ingredient in a great variety of starters and main dishes.

## Selecting tomatoes for indoor growing

In order to grow tomatoes within the limited space of small containers, you must select the hybrids specially developed by seedsmen for the purpose. It is no use buying seed, or established pot-grown plants, of varieties which are genetically programmed to thrive best in open outdoor situations. In the open garden they can spread out, put down long root systems and grow tall in the sunlight. A number of the most popular garden varieties put up a very poor show indeed in restricted spaces and in an indoor environment.

Purpose-bred F1 hybrids are ideal for indoor growing. The seeds are a little more expensive, but the results make the initial outlay well worth while. My first choice is Pixie, a fast-growing, compact variety which thrives in pots and window boxes, tubs and hanging baskets. It is equally happy on an inside window-edge or outside on the patio or balcony. It produces many trusses of small, firm, sweet and juicy fruits. Tiny Tim is another attractive small-fruited variety, grown in the same way as Pixie. This may be quite difficult to obtain, and appears to have been superseded by more recently developed small tomatoes. If you can find it, look out also for the yellow-fruiting form.

Another cultivar of the same type is the Cherry Tomato, which produces large quantities of smaller fruits, each about 1in (2.5cm) in

---

### CULTIVATION CHECKLIST

Sow seed thinly into moist growing medium in large seed trays; allow the seeds to germinate in gentle warmth, 60-65°F (15-18°C)

— • —

Remove covering when a few seedlings show above the soil surface

— • —

Pot seedlings individually in 3in (8cm) pots when they have developed three pairs of true leaves

— • —

Move containers to a warm, bright location and keep the seedlings well watered

— • —

Pot on into 5in (13cm) or 7in (17cm) pots, depending upon size

— • —

Support with canes, tying in the main stems

— • —

As flowers form, feed every 10 days with tomato fertilizer; as flowers open, spray daily for several days to disperse pollen

— • —

Remove side shoots and control size if necessary by pinching out the main growing point, allowing each plant to form 4-5 trusses

— • —

Harvest when the tomatoes are of the required size and color diameter. These, too, are firm-textured and have a sweet, fresh flavor.

Small Fry is an American cultivar producing plants growing to 30in (75cm) in height, with cherry-sized, very sweet fruits which mature within about 65 days of germination. A smaller plant, and earlier-cropping tomato, is Early Salad Hybrid – at only 12in (30cm) tall, this is ideal for indoor gardeners with very restricted growing space. A type suitable for autumn harvesting, since it takes 70 days to mature, is Hybrid Patio, offering medium-sized tomatoes on a plant between 24in (60cm) and 30in (75cm) high.

All these mini-tomatoes provide more fruits in proportion to the available space than the older-established varieties, but if you need a larger variety for slicing, select from Eurocross, Supercross and Moneycross, all of which are indoor cultivars.

The yellow-skinned varieties best for small-space growing are Golden Sunrise and Golden Queen. Many people harbor the suspicion that unless a tomato is red it is not ripe, but the yellow-skinned cultivars are commonly found to taste sweeter than many of the red tomatoes because they are less acid. Their skins are also much thinner.

The length of time from germination to flowering of these cultivars (unless otherwise stated) is on average about 52 days in optimum conditions. If you have the space, take the opportunity to grow more than one variety. This enables you to get to know their cultivation requirements and gives you a choice in both appearance and flavor for use in salads or cooked dishes.

## Sowing tomato seed

Growing tomatoes from seed is a more economical method than growing established potted plants. It may seem that buying plants saves time and, initially, leaves more room for growing other crops, but they are generally not available until quite late in the season, whereas you can sow seed quite early in the year indoors, from early to mid spring, and control the cropping to your requirements.

Sow the seed in large, flat containers, such as the largest size of flat seed trays. Make sure these are quite clean, if you have used them previously for other plants. Use a peat-based growing medium – a proprietary brand or your own mixture – and firm the surface of the filled tray lightly. The medium should be damp but not wet. Sow the seed as thinly as possible; tomato seeds are quite large, so it is easy to space them out evenly, about 1in (2.5cm) apart. (If you have difficulty handling the seeds, use a pair of tweezers.) Sprinkle a thin layer of moist growing medium over the top, just covering the seeds.

Place the seed trays in the warmest situation you can provide. A wide, sunny windowsill is ideal. Be careful where you position the trays in relation to fires and central heating appliances. An unnaturally high temperature dries out the growing medium so the seeds cannot germinate. They need only gentle warmth and moderate but steady moisture. A temperature between 60°F (16°C) and 65°F (18°C) is sufficient.

Cover the seed trays with pieces of black plastic to exclude light until germination occurs, but do not tuck in the plastic sheets at the sides. This prevents free circulation of air, encouraging mould which will destroy the seeds. Ventilation is essential.

Tomato seeds take about nine days to germinate; but there is always some individual variation, so lift the cover to see how they are progressing from about the seventh day onwards. Gradually the surface of the compost is disturbed by the upward thrust of the germinating shoots. As soon as the first two or three are through, remove the covering and allow the seedlings to adjust gradually to full light. Spray them very lightly with tepid water from a fine hand-spray.

**Indoor/outdoor growing**
Keep tomato plants indoors until late spring or early summer; they must at no time be exposed to very low temperatures or frosty conditions. Cherry tomatoes can be planted up in hanging baskets outdoors in summer.

Stand young tomato plants on a pebble tray to allow water to drain freely out of the pots.

## Growing on

The seedlings grow apace and should be watered gently as soon as the surface of the growing medium feels dry, before the seedlings show any signs of wilting. After the cotyledons or 'seed leaves' appear the first true leaves are produced. As soon as the plants have two or three pairs of these, they are ready to be transplanted into individual 3in (8cm) pots. At this stage they will appreciate a 'stronger' potting medium, such as a soil-based mixture with added plant nutrients.

Keep the soil well-watered, but not wet. It is useful to stand the pots on a tray of pebbles, so that excess water can drain freely out of the pots. The damp pebbles then keep the surrounding atmosphere nicely moist.

When the plants have produced sufficient growth to be transplanted into larger pots they should ideally go straight into the containers in which the plants will flower and set fruit. This shows another advantage of having chosen the small cultivars in the first place: there is no need to find space for a multitude of large pots. Pixie can be grown successfully in 5in (13cm) pots: the larger cultivars do well in 7in (17cm) pots. Hanging baskets can be planted with a single tomato plant or more than one, depending upon size: cherry tomatoes look particularly attractive trailing from a basket in a sunny window.

Site your tomato plants in the warmest and brightest location you can provide. A sunny position is half the battle, and the plants will reward you with masses of fruit.

I have been asked whether grow-bags can be recommended for tomatoes. These are very useful in a greenhouse or small garden, but indoors are uneconomical of space. You cannot grow more than four plants in one standard-size bag – 40×15×15in (110×38×38cm). In a space that size you can site six 7in (18cm) pots lengthways and two pots widthways – a total of twelve plants individually potted. If your area for indoor gardening is limited, this comparison speaks for itself.

## Supporting and training

The young plants should be supported with canes or tomato sticks, which need not be more than 12in (30cm) long for most of these small cultivars. When you are potting on tomatoes into their final containers, insert the canes into the growing medium before transferring the plants, to avoid damaging the roots. Tie in the plant stems immediately with garden twine or plastic-covered wire ties to keep them upright. If allowed to grow on unsupported, the stems may distort and become weakened.

Certain varieties need side-stopping, which means removing the small shoots which appear in the leaf axils. The bush cultivars, such as the trailing varieties suitable for growing in hanging baskets, do not need this treatment. You can control the overall size of the smaller cultivars by pinching out the main growing point when the plants have achieved a suitable size. This encourages them to form more trusses, so serves a dual purpose.

## Fruiting and harvest

As soon as the plants reach the flowering stage they should be fed every 10 days with a balanced tomato food. The small all-female hybrid plants are self-pollinating, but if you are growing traditional varieties which would normally be pollinated outdoors by the bees, you will have to make sure that pollination takes place. A simple method of doing this is to take a fine hand-spray and lightly spray the flowers every day for a few days. This distributes the pollen from the ripe anthers, and spreading the operation over several days ensures that unripe anthers are treated as they mature.

Provide extra support for the plants as the trusses start to form, with an additional cane for each stem if necessary, as the trusses can become very heavy as the fruits ripen. From this point, feed the plants every five

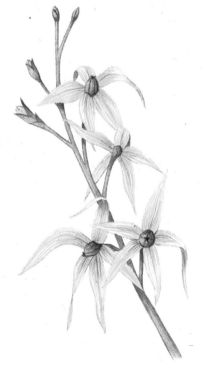

days; they are putting so much energy into forming fruits that they need all the nutrients they can get. Four or five trusses are as many as a single plant should be expected to produce, so pinch out any additional growing points to concentrate the plant's energies into the existing trusses. The plant's main growing point should be nipped out now, for the same reason, if you have not done this before.

Continue to supply water to the containers liberally as the fruits swell and ripen, particularly during the height of summer when conditions are hot and dry. Do not be tempted to increase the feed supplied to the plants in the hope of encouraging a better crop; excessive doses of fertilizer are more likely to cause the fruits to split.

You can harvest at any stage as the fruits mature, depending upon the colour and size preferred. Early harvesting encourages the plants to set more fruit, and the tomatoes will continue to ripen after picking if taken before they have fully turned red.

# RADISHES

The radish is the quickest of vegetables to
mature and should be harvested while at
the peak of crisp freshness. They are
delicious eaten raw, as an appetizer or in
salad, and can also be lightly cooked –
boiled, steamed or stir-fried.

**R**adishes are a rewarding crop for first-time gardeners because they show results quickly and are quite easy to grow. You can harvest a regular crop of radishes from a series of medium-depth, shallow containers with very little toil or trouble, provided that you choose the right varieties for indoor growing. They have good dietary value since they contain iron and other useful nutrients. Radishes are perhaps best eaten fresh, for their crisp texture and lightly peppery flavor. For serving hot, they should be cooked as gently as possible to preserve these qualities and their nutritional value.

## Selecting radishes for indoor growing

Globe cultivars give the best results in container growing, because globe radishes require less vertical root space than the long tapering types. Cherry Belle has a sweet, mild taste and stays in harvestable condition for a long time without rotting or becoming woody, so if the crop does well you can pull the radishes at your leisure. Red Prince is another good all-red radish, while Sparkler is an attractive red-and-white globe radish which can be recommended.

It is possible to grow the longer types of radish in containers – French Breakfast is a popular choice – but these must be planted in tubs to allow for the deeper rooting, so the crop will occupy a greater space.

## Sowing and germination

Radishes like a high proportion of humus in the soil, which can very easily be provided by crumbling dried, dead leaves between your fingers and working them into the potting mixture. This creates the best medium for raising radishes, but it is not essential: if you do not have the opportunity to provide the leafy material, a satisfactory crop will be obtained by using a peat-based growing medium or adding a little peat to

---

**CULTIVATION CHECKLIST**

Sow seed into moist, peat-based or humus-enriched potting medium; maintain a temperature of 60-65°F (15-18°C) during germination

— • —

As seedlings appear, provide a light position and keep the growing medium moist

— • —

Thin seedlings to allow 1in (2.5cm) between plants

— • —

Pull radishes for use as soon as they reach the required size; harvest 3-4 weeks after sowing

---

**Indoor/outdoor growing**
Radishes can be sown in containers outdoors or grown on from indoor sowings from late spring. The requirement for frequent watering should not be neglected.

a soil-based mixture. Acid conditions, however, are unsuitable for this crop, so if your potting mixture tends to be acid, apply a small quantity of garden lime to neutralize it or work in some finely crushed eggshells.

Radishes do not like to grow in compacted or lumpy soil, so before sowing break up and moisten the surface layer of the growing medium and then press it down gently to make an even bed for the seeds.

Radish seeds are spherical and extremely small. It is impossible to space them out as they are sown, but they should be sown as thinly as possible. Moisten the growing medium lightly before sowing and cover the scattered seed with a fine layer of soil.

To obtain a continuous supply, practise succession sowing at three-to-four-week intervals. Radishes can be started at any time for indoor growing. Germination takes about four to seven days.

## Growing on

As the seedlings appear, the weaker ones can be pulled to make space for the others to develop. There is no need to waste any space in the containers; 1in (2.5cm) between the plants allows room for the globes to expand. If you have opted to grow the larger types of radish, judge the growing space according to the size of the particular variety.

Radishes do not like excessive heat or sun. Position the plants in good light but protected from direct sun, especially during the hottest part of the day in summer. Keep the containers well watered to encourage quick growth and succulent, sweet, mild globes. There is no need to use liquid fertilizers as the crop is fast-maturing. For best results, the radishes must be provided with conditions conducive to rapid growth. If they are held back by low temperatures or lack of moisture, the globes will not form and the plants will 'bolt' (run to seed).

Pull the radishes for use as soon as they are ready; if left too long the texture can deteriorate, becoming coarse and woody.

# LETTUCES

*There is nothing better than a crisp, fresh lettuce as the basis of a salad or as a side dish to accompany meat, egg and pasta dishes. Indoor cultivation provides an extended season of home-grown produce.*

Lettuces for indoor growing can be divided into three main categories – cabbage (head) lettuce, cos (romaine) lettuce and non-hearting loose-leaf types, also called salad bowl varieties. I recommend growing some of each kind, if space allows. This provides the greatest variation of taste and texture. Lettuce, like most other green vegetables, starts to lose its vitamin content almost as soon as it has been cut, so not only do you obtain the best flavor from lettuce culled only minutes before eating, it also contributes more goodness to your diet.

With experience, it will become apparent how much seed to sow at one time to produce the size of crop which you can readily use while it is still in the best condition. However, if early efforts result in a glut of lettuces, don't forget that it can be eaten cooked – lightly boiled, stir-fried with other vegetables, or made into a cool-tasting soup. Once you have established a good crop, it is worth checking recipe books to find out how versatile lettuce can be as an ingredient of hot and cold dishes. The golden rule is not to overcook, by whatever method, as cooking destroys the nutrients very quickly.

## Selecting lettuces for indoor growing

There is a great variety of lettuces and your choice may depend to some extent upon the space which you wish to give to this particular crop. Little Gem is an excellent cos lettuce which matures quickly and has a sweet taste. In the open garden, this can grow to quite a size; in containers indoors it does not achieve such size and is a manageable and productive plant. If you have room to grow lettuces in large tubs, there is a larger cos, Lobjoit's Green, which has a crisp texture and rich colour, a popular gardener's choice worth trying for container growing.

Among the cabbage lettuces, my recommended varieties for indoor growing are Tom Thumb and All the Year Round. Tom Thumb is a nicely compact plant, fast to mature and well flavored. All the Year

### CULTIVATION CHECKLIST

Sow seed in trays in early spring

— • —

As seedlings develop, thin to 6in (15cm) apart

— • —

Place the plants in a light, moderately warm location and water generously throughout the growing period

— • —

After 6 weeks include a liquid feed in the watering every 10 days

— • —

Harvest hearted plants when a firm heart has formed; start to crop from loose-leaved types as soon as leaves are of a suitable size

The three main types of lettuce for indoor growing are cos, cabbage or head lettuce, and loose-leaf or salad bowl varieties.

Round is a medium-sized lettuce less likely than others to bolt (run to seed) if you forget to water for a short period. Bibb is an American variety which takes 65 days to mature and is of a good size for container growing.

Loose-leaf varieties include the green and red salad bowl varieties which produce a more open habit of growth without central hearting. You can simply pick the leaves a few at a time as they are needed. The red-tinged leaves are a pleasant variation for inclusion in mixed salads.

## Sowing and germination

Indoors, you can start lettuces from seed as winter turns to spring. Even All the Year Round, despite its name, cannot be expected to produce a perfect crop during dark days with the risk of low night-time temperatures, but if you can provide stable conditions and the brightest possible location, it is worth trying a late autumn sowing which will produce a winter harvest.

Lettuces are undemanding as to soil type, but this does not mean you should sow in a poor quality potting mixture or recycle exhausted soil. If you have a garden, an economical growing medium is garden soil sifted together with a commercially produced potting mixture. Peat is not necessary, but a small amount of sand can be added to aid drainage. Alternatively, you can simply use a commercial soil-based or universal potting medium, or any mixture of your own which has produced successful results with other crops.

Unlike some other vegetables, lettuces do not need a great depth of soil, since their roots are not very long. Shallow containers can be used, and standard seed trays are adequate for sowing and growing on the plants. But do not crowd a lot of seedlings together in a small tray; the smaller lettuce varieties should be thinned or transplanted to about 6in

(15cm) apart. If you are growing the larger types, such as Lobjoit's Green, provide deeper containers and more lateral space for the plants to develop.

The soil should be just moist when the seeds are sown. Fill the trays and firm the soil lightly; then spray very sparingly with tepid water from a hand-spray. Lettuce seeds are quite small, so do not waste time trying to space them evenly as you sow – the seedlings can be thinned out later. Scatter the seed thinly and cover with a fine layer of the potting mixture, about ¼in (5mm) deep. If you have very little space and want to avoid any wastage, you can sow pelleted seeds which can be placed accurately at intervals across the soil surface; however, this is a more expensive way of buying seed, and you will have fewer plants for your money. Packets of loose seed are comparatively better value as you can make several small succession sowings from one packet.

## Growing on

When the seedlings are large enough to handle, thin out the weaklings or transplant a proportion of them into other containers leaving the required space for the remaining plants to grow on. Alternatively, the seedlings can all be left to grow larger and the thinnings can be taken when they are at a suitable size to provide very tender young leaves for salad use; but don't leave this so late that the remaining plants are inhibited from maturing to full size.

Lettuces take from eight to twelve weeks to come to maturity, depending on the cultivar and the growing conditions. They require a good deal of water and quickly wilt if deprived of adequate moisture. Keep them in mild or warm conditions; being tender-leaved, lettuces should not be exposed to strong sunshine when grown indoors, as there is the risk of scorching. If they grow in a window which receives full sun all day, shade the plants with newspaper or draw the curtains

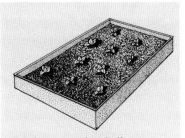

Sow lettuce seed in shallow trays and thin out the seedlings to provide adequate space for the young plants to develop.

**Indoor/outdoor growing**
Start lettuces from seed in containers outdoors after all spring frosts have passed. Indoor-sown plants can be moved to an outside windowsill or to the patio or balcony from mid spring onwards.

temporarily while the sun is at its height.

Water the young plants regularly to keep the soil moist. As the lettuces become well established, a good soaking does more good than continual sprinklings of water, as the moisture must reach the finest branches of the root system and carry nutrients from the growing medium to the extremities of the roots. After about six weeks of growth, the plants benefit from a liquid feed every ten days or so. Overfeeding does not encourage more rapid growth; strong doses of fertilizer do more harm than good, so check the manufacturer's instructions on dilution of the fertilizer.

Lettuces are highly attractive to slugs and snails, so be vigilant if you leave the windows open or stand the plants outside during fine weather. Check the plants, the soil surface and the outside of the container to make sure there are no damaging pests attached.

## Harvesting

Cut cabbage and cos lettuces when a firm heart has formed but take note that it is the darker colored outer leaves which contain the most minerals and other nutrients, so don't discard these. Trim off any bruised or discolored sections and cut or shred the remainder for inclusion in salads. Harvest the leaves of loose-leaved varieties as and when they are needed; continual small cullings encourage production of new growth.

# LAND CRESS

*The fresh texture and 'hot' flavor of land cress make it an appetizing addition to salad, where it contrasts with the coolness of lettuce and cucumbers. For the indoor gardener, this is a practical alternative to watercress.*

L and cress is similar in appearance and flavor to watercress, but it is easier to grow and certainly better suited to cultivation in containers. Watercress is an aquatic plant, which should ideally be grown in running water – clearly a difficult prospect for indoor gardening. For comparable rich color and distinctive sharp flavor in salads, land cress is an excellent substitute which can be grown through a long season under indoor conditions. It can be used in all the same ways as watercress: it makes a well-flavored soup and can be cooked as a hot vegetable like spinach, and of course is a pleasing garnish for meals and snacks.

## Selecting land cress for indoor growing

This is not a vegetable with a wide range of varieties, but it may be offered under different names. Land cress is of European origin, but has become naturalized in America, and is also known as American cress and as Belle Isle cress. The plant is low-growing with a rosette formation of spreading, dark green leaves. The color is maintained through autumn and winter cropping.

## Sowing and germination

A rich and moisture-retentive soil is needed for growing land cress. Incorporate some humus – commercially prepared or made by crumbling dried leaves (see page 17) – or well-rotted manure in the potting mixture.

Sow the seed in seed trays and cover with soil to a depth of no more than ½in (1cm). The seeds are given a head start if you soak them in water overnight before sowing. Maintain a temperature in the range 50-60°F (10-15°C) during germination. Land cress is not a demanding crop, but in common with other indoor vegetables, requires warmth and gentle moisture during the initial stages. As the seedlings appear,

---

**CULTIVATION CHECKLIST**

Sow seed in trays and allow to germinate at 50-60°F (10-15°F)

— • —

Pot on into individual pots or large containers at 6in (15cm) apart

— • —

Position plants in a bright but not sunny location and keep well watered

— • —

Harvest when leaves are of a useful size, taking a few leaves from each plant at one time

---

**Indoor/outdoor growing**
Land cress can be moved outside when all frosts have passed. Make sure that the potting mixture is kept permanently moist.

move the containers to a bright, but not sunny, position.

To obtain a continuous supply, make small succession sowings from early spring onwards. Batches sown through late summer and early autumn provide fresh leaves into the winter months.

## Growing on

Thin out the seedlings as they develop so that they are not weakened by overcrowding. When they are large enough to handle, pot them on into individual pots, or into troughs or tubs at about 6in (15cm) apart.

Continuous moisture is essential to the success of this crop. The plants should be encouraged to grow quickly – the period from sowing to harvest is only about eight weeks – and moist conditions are conducive to rapid growth. Provided that the growing medium is of good quality and contains adequate nutrients, it should not be necessary to supply a fertilizer.

In hot, dry conditions, the plants may run rapidly to seed and the flavour of the leaves becomes harsh when this happens. Do not expose the land cress to strong sunlight, which causes it to bolt. Keep plants partially shaded or position them at a window which receives good light but no direct sun.

You can start to harvest the leaves as soon as they are of sufficient size and quantity to be useful in the kitchen. Land cress can be treated as a cut-and-come-again crop. Take only a few leaves from each plant at one time, to encourage further growth.

# MELONS

*These exotic-looking plants may be thought difficult to grow, but appearances can be deceptive. Following the procedure given here, you will be able to harvest melons five months from the germination of the seed.*

**W**hether you eat melon as a starter, a salad ingredient or a dessert, for the keen indoor gardener, this is an irresistible challenge. Melons belong to the same family of plants as the cucumber, the Cucurbitaceae, and need plenty of warmth and light to grow well and produce fruit. As with the more common of indoor food crops, the element which puts you on the path to success is selection of suitable cultivars for indoor growing. This means choosing the smaller-fruited kinds which can develop fully in limited growing space.

## Selecting melons for indoor growing

Canteloupe and Ogen melon varieties are well-suited to cultivation in containers. A cultivar known as Ogen 339 gives excellent results, and either of the F1 hybrids Sweetheart and Joy is also a good choice. The latter is said to be highly disease-resistant, although the fungal diseases to which melons are susceptible are most likely to infect a large crop and there is less danger of disease in a small indoor container-grown melon patch. Some melon plants are quite tall-growing; dwarf varieties may be the most suitable for the growing area you can provide.

An American cultivar called Minnesota Midget is early-maturing and, as the name implies, takes up less space than some other varieties. This is a canteloupe, a vigorous little plant producing plenty of small fruits, each about 4in (10cm) across, with sweet orange flesh.

## Sowing and germination

Sow the seeds on edge, one per 3in (8cm) pot. They seem to thrive best in ordinary peat-based potting medium. The seed should not be buried too deep – ¾in (2cm) is just right. Cover the seed very thinly with soil and water with a fine spray. Place the pots in a warm location, cover them with a sheet of newspaper and place a sheet of glass over the top.

The time it takes for the seeds to germinate depends upon the degree

Keep melon seed covered with a sheet of newspaper and glass until germination occurs and the seedlings start to show.

**Staying in**
Melon plants require warm, moist conditions throughout their development and are best grown indoors where temperature and humidity can be controlled.

73

of warmth; at temperatures of 65°F (18°C) or more, you should see results within several days. If the seeds are sown very early in the spring, they are best kept in a heated propagator at a steady heat, minimum 75°F (24°C): otherwise wait until late spring before sowing. Cool conditions inhibit or prevent germination.

When the new growth shows above the soil, remove the glass and paper coverings and place the containers in a warm, bright place. Keep the developing seedlings in a moist atmosphere by spraying around them. Do not overwater the soil, but do not allow it to dry out; it should be kept evenly moist.

## Growing on

When the seedlings have produced four true leaves, following the appearance of the seed leaves, they should be potted on into larger pots. Melons do not like to be potted on continually, so at this stage you should move them to the pots in which they can develop and mature. The size of pot depends upon the cultivar which you have selected, but I have had good results using 7in (18cm) pots.

Site the plants in the sunniest position available – a window which receives sun all day is ideal – and keep the plants well watered. The moist atmosphere must also be maintained – humidity is essential to healthy growth. Spray the plants lightly on a regular basis; in hot, dry conditions, spraying should be a daily task.

## Training maturing plants

As the plants grow, train the main stem against a cane, tying it in firmly. When the plant has reached the maximum height, in the case of dwarf cultivars, or up to 6ft (1.8m) if you are growing a regular variety, pinch out the growing point. This will have the effect of making the plant produce side shoots (laterals), the fruit-bearing sub-stems.

---

### CULTIVATION CHECKLIST

Sow seeds singly, on edge, in 3in (8cm) pots; cover pots with newspaper and a sheet of glass

— • —

Keep the growing medium moist and maintain a minimum temperature of 60°F (15°C)

— • —

Pot on into 7in (17cm) pots when the plants have developed four true leaves

— • —

Site the containers in a sunny location and water generously; spray daily during hot weather

— • —

Train the main plant stems on canes; pinch out growing points to encourage lateral growth

— • —

Train laterals on wires stretched horizontally between canes

— • —

Hand-pollinate female flowers when fully open, except on all-female hybrids

— • —

Pinch out shoots leaving one leaf beyond the fruit; feed plants with liquid fertilizer every ten days

— • —

Support developing fruits with nets secured above the plant growth; reduce humidity as fruits ripen

— • —

Harvest when fruits are fully ripe and fragrant

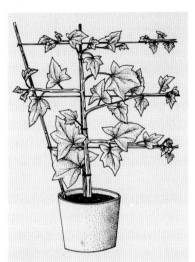

Support melon plants horizontally as well as vertically, on canes and wires.

The laterals are most productive if trained horizontally to the growing axis. However limited your growing area, try to provide a structure of horizontal wires secured to vertical canes set in the pots at the outer ends of your row of plants. This will produce the best fruit crop.

When the laterals have reached about 18in (45cm) in length, pinch out their growing points. This discourages them from producing further leafy growth and concentrates their energy into developing sturdy growth for fruit-bearing. By the time the plants have reached this stage, the flowers should be budding.

## Fruiting and harvest

As the flowers open, you should attend to pollinating the plants if necessary. All-female hybrids are self-fertile and need no pollination. Other varieties need to be pollinated by hand, using a soft brush to transfer the pollen from the male to the female flower (see page 23). Carry out pollination in full sun, in the middle of the day, when the blooms are fully open. Do not spray the plants immediately beforehand – the pollen should not be moist. It is a good idea to repeat hand-pollination on two or three days in succession, pollinating four female flowers on each plant at the same time. This method encourages the fruits to swell and ripen evenly.

As the fruits start to swell visibly, pinch out the tips of the growing shoots at a point leaving one leaf beyond the fruit. At this stage, feed the plants with a suitable liquid fertilizer, diluted according to the manufacturer's instructions. Water in a liquid feed every ten days; keep up the watering of the potting medium and continue spraying to provide a humid atmosphere. On days when the sun is particularly intense, shade the plants with a sheet of newspaper placed inside the window to prevent the sun from 'cooking' the fruits.

When the fruits have swelled to tennis-ball size, they should be

75

Use net bags to support the ripening fruit, so their weight does not cause damage to the plant.

supported with nets. Various types of fine netting are available at garden supply centers; alternatively, you can save the net bags in which vegetable produce is sometimes sold in markets and stores. Thread a length of string through the mesh at the top of the bag to form a drawstring (if using a piece of garden netting, do the same at the bottom edge and secure it to form a bag). Place the net bag around the fruit and tie the string firmly. Secure it above the plant so that the fruit is supported. If there is no suitable framework to which the strings can be tied, you will need to fix a wooden batten fitted with a row of hooks above the plants. The netting supports are important, as the increasing weight of the fruit can cause stems to snap, when the fruit will fall and become bruised or split.

Reduce the humidity while the fruits are ripening; stop spraying the air around the plants and provide water to the soil in the pots only. Make sure there is adequate ventilation allowing free circulation of air around the plants.

You will know when the melons are fully ripe and ready to eat – they will fill the room with a strong, sweet fragrance.

# INDOOR VEGETABLE CROPS

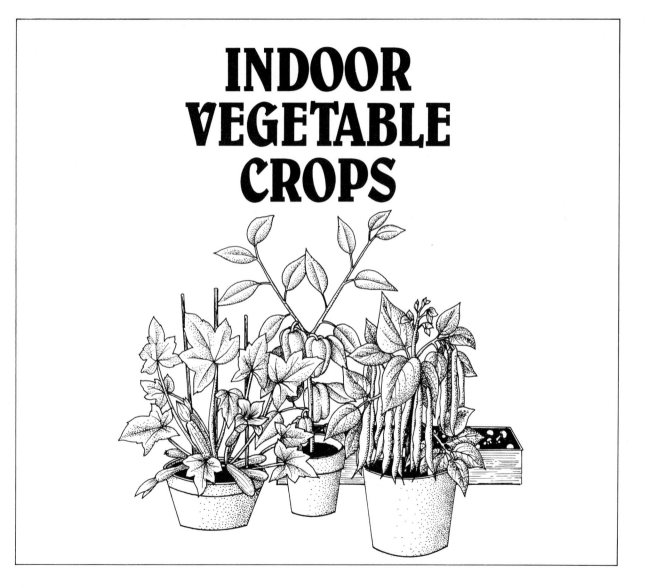

# PEPPERS

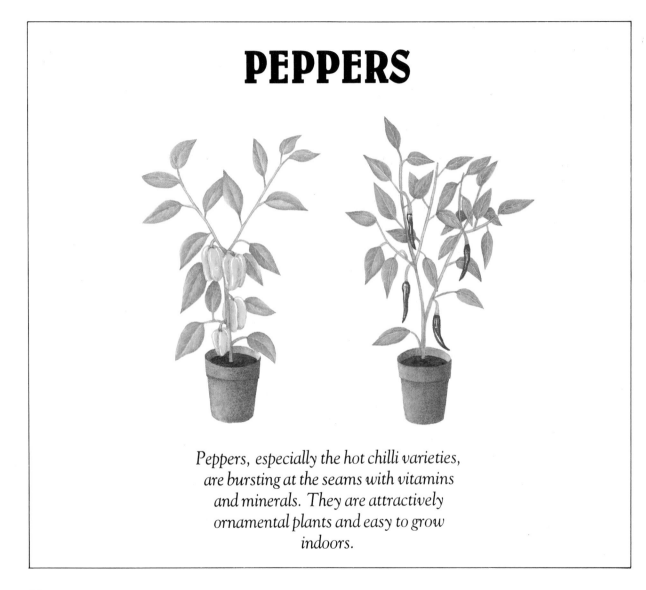

*Peppers, especially the hot chilli varieties, are bursting at the seams with vitamins and minerals. They are attractively ornamental plants and easy to grow indoors.*

Peppers are of two kinds, the large sweet peppers which can be sliced into salads, cooked as a stuffed vegetable or included in a variety of hot dishes, and the small, hot chilli peppers which are used as seasoning and to add bite to spiced and curried foods. The red, green and yellow peppers which you have seen on sale are not different varieties; they are three stages in the ripening process of the same fruit. Green is the first stage, turning to a brilliant yellow before finally becoming red. The peppers continue to ripen after picking, and harvesting them early increases the productivity of the plant. If you pick peppers at the green stage, these will develop yellow and red coloring while new green peppers are forming on the plant. This gives you the variety of color so attractive in salads while encouraging the plants to produce the most plentiful crop.

## Selecting sweet peppers

Both all-female hybrids and non-hybrid types of sweet peppers can be recommended for indoor growing. The variety producing the largest fruits, ideal for stuffed pepper recipes, is Big Bertha F1 hybrid. The peppers from this variety can grow to 10in (25cm) long and 4in (10cm) across. It is an early-cropping hybrid, needing plenty of sun for satisfactory results. For fruits of a smaller size, but more of them on the plant, choose Canape, another F1 hybrid. This one has been bred to be cold-resistant, which does not mean that it will thrive, or even survive, in normally unfavorable conditions. It still needs a high germination temperature, but will do better than some other cultivars if there is a low quota of sunshine during the growing season, or at times when even the indoor temperature is none too warm.

The American variety Twiggy has been promoted with the slogan 'You can eat it like an apple, it's so sweet'. Should it not be to your taste to do so, Twiggy still is recommended as a tasty and succulent pepper,

---

### CULTIVATION CHECKLIST

Sow two or three seeds to a 3in (8cm) pot and maintain a temperature of 75°F (24°C)

— · —

Move containers to a warm, sunny location as seedlings emerge; maintain average daytime temperature of 70°F (21°C), night-time minimum 55°F (13°C)

— · —

Pot on singly into 7in (17cm) pots when plants have produced two pairs of true leaves

— · —

Water frequently to keep the growing medium moist

— · —

Support with canes as growth increases

— · —

Spray plants regularly to maintain humidity and provide a liquid feed every 10 days from the time when flower buds begin to form

— · —

Carry out pollination as necessary to set fruit

— · —

Harvest when fruits are of usable size

**Staying in**
Peppers require a protected, warm, sunny location and a controlled supply of moisture to the growing medium. They are not suited to outdoor growing.

an early cropper with the fruits all forming at the top of the plant, making for a quick and easy harvest. Another very sweet, luscious and thick-skinned variety is Gold Star, which has been so bred that it stays yellow as it finally ripens. This is an excellent and colorful choice for use in salads.

It may be useful to start with a seed pack of mixed F1 varieties, such as Summer Salad Mixed, to introduce you to the various types. This includes thick- and thin-walled varieties, some early croppers and others bred to develop through the normal growing season. These different ripening times are another way of enabling you to have peppers of different colors all at the same time, an enlivening touch for both raw and cooked vegetable dishes.

## Selecting chilli peppers

These much smaller peppers are used only for flavoring, specifically in the hot and spicy foods of Asian cookery. Using fresh chillies is vastly preferable to using them dried, but the flavor is much more intense, so halve the quantity in a recipe where dried chillies are given in the ingredients list. Handle them carefully and use them sparingly in your cooking until you have become accustomed to their strength, and do not be tempted to taste the raw chilli pepper while you are preparing food. Ripened red chillies are even stronger than those at the green stage. Nutritionally, chillies are a useful addition to your diet; tests have shown that they are rich in iron, potassium, B vitamins and vitamin C.

Big Jim, which is not an F1 hybrid, is a good choice for pot cultivation. Three or four plants will produce a huge crop, some of which can be dried for use later when the harvest is over. This plant can, and often does, grow to 4ft (1.2m) tall, and must be supported accordingly. The F1 hybrid El Cid crops more prolifically than Big Jim, but produces smaller fruits – about 1½in (4cm) long, with a hotter flavor.

## Sowing and germination

Sweet peppers and chillies are grown in the same way. The seeds need a minimum temperature of 75°F (24°C) to germinate, and the growing plants require plenty of sun and warmth if they are to flower, set seed and produce fruits.

If you can maintain the high temperature for germination, you can start seeds as early as late winter or early spring; if temperatures are variable, wait until mid spring. Sow in 3in (8cm) pots, using a good-quality potting medium containing some peat. Two or three seeds can be sown in a pot of this size. Germination may take 14 days or longer even with the ideal degree of warmth, so do not expect instant results.

As the seedlings appear, place them in the lightest and warmest position you can provide. When the seedlings have produced two pairs of true leaves, pot them on into separate pots. A 7in (17cm) pot is adequate space for a single plant. Keep the growing medium moist, but not wet.

## Growing on

The high temperature needed for germination does not have to be maintained throughout the growing period. The warmer the situation, the better the progress of the plants, and they should not be exposed to temperatures lower than 55°F (13°C), even at night. Aim for a daytime average of 70°F (21°C) and make sure the pots are sited where the plants can enjoy all the available sunshine during the day. Water moderately but frequently; it is important never to let the potting mixture dry out, since the warm atmosphere has a drying effect.

As the plants' growth increases, provide each one with a cane as support and tie in the stems firmly. Peppers have an upright habit of growth, but the tall, heavy-cropping varieties must have this support. Smaller-growing types may not need this precaution throughout their

Place developing plants in a sunny, warm position and keep the growing medium continuously moist.

development, but it may be advisable in the final stages as the weight of the fruit develops.

## Fruiting and harvest

When the flower buds start to form, spray the plants with a fine hand-spray and provide a liquid feed every 10 days. If you are growing F1 hybrids, no pollination is required. For other varieties, spray lightly two or three days in succession as the flowers open to spread the pollen, or hand-pollinate the plants with a soft brush, as described on page 23. Peppers seem remarkably free of pests and diseases, so there should be no problems on that score.

You can start to harvest the green fruits when they are of reasonable size, for immediate use or for ripening away from the plant, or you can allow them to change color on the plant, but do not leave them so long that they lose their sweet succulence.

# FRENCH BEANS

*French beans, also called dwarf beans or
bush beans, are an extremely useful bean
crop for container growing. They take up
little space and produce a high reward
because there is absolutely no waste – the
pods are eaten whole.*

**Indoor/outdoor growing**
French beans can be placed outside on a patio or balcony in late spring when the young plants have developed sturdy growth.

**CULTIVATION CHECKLIST**

Sow seed in early spring at 3in (8cm) apart for potting on, or 6in (15cm) apart if growing on in the same container

— • —

Place seedlings in a sunny location; pot on as necessary into 6in (15cm) pots or into tubs or troughs at 6in (15cm) apart

— • —

Supply moisture to the soil and maintain a humid atmosphere around the plants

— • —

When flowers appear, spray regularly to disperse pollen

— • —

Feed with liquid fertilizer every 10-12 days as beanpods form

— • —

Harvest as soon as a useful crop is ready

The sweet flavor of French beans is unlike that of any other type of bean. Being completely stringless, they can be picked while young to be thinly sliced and eaten raw, but it is more usual to grow them on to full size and lightly boil or steam them for serving as a side vegetable. If you harvest a serving quantity and cook them immediately, none of the flavor and nutritional content is lost between picking and cooking. Unlike runner and broad beans, which become coarse with age and excessive size, these dwarf varieties stay beautifully sweet, tender and delicious on the plant. Another distinct advantage is that the more you pick, the more the plant continues to produce – it is not unusual to be able to gather at least four crops from one plant, given the right growing conditions.

## Selecting French beans for indoor growing

The smallest cultivars suitable for growing indoors in limited space are Limelight and Royal Burgundy, which both reach a height of about 12in (30cm). Royal Burgundy may slightly exceed this if conditions are to its liking. It produces round beanpods; Limelight is a flat-podded variety.

## Sowing and germination

French beans require a well-drained soil with a little lime. They must be grown in containers with drainage holes in the bottom; solid containers with crockery shards or gravel at the base do not allow for sufficient drainage. A growing mixture of soil, peat, sand and humus is to be specially recommended for these beans, although a commercially produced soil-based compost is an acceptable alternative. In either case, increase the lime content by sprinkling on and mixing in a little powdered garden lime or, if you favor making use of kitchen waste, add a small amount of finely pulverized eggshells.

Bean seeds are large and easy to handle; these can be sown 6in (15cm) apart in a seed tray or trough.

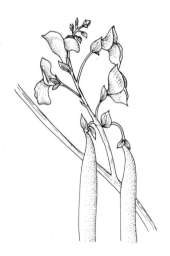

Start the beans in containers large enough to allow 3in (8cm) between the young plants if you plan to pot them into larger containers, or 6in (15cm) apart if you sow them direct into the container in which they will mature. Make a hole 2in (5cm) deep in the soil mixture and insert one seed. Fill the hole and repeat the process according to the size of the pot or trough. It is important with this type of bean not to firm the surface of the soil too vigorously. A hard surface will impede germination or prevent it altogether.

Beans for indoor growing can be started in early spring, but they react badly to low soil temperature, so maintain a minimum of 50-54°F (10-12°C). As the seedlings appear, move them to a sunny location and transplant to larger containers, if necessary, when a few true leaves have formed.

## Growing on

Keep the soil moist but not wet and provide a humid atmosphere around the growing plants. Plenty of sunshine is beneficial, but protect plants from fierce heat by shielding them with newspaper when the sun is at its height. When the plants are well established in their containers they will put on a growth spurt and soon produce flower buds. At this stage, spray the plants regularly to make sure pollen is dispersed as the flowers open; this will encourage them to set good pods.

The pods begin to form as the flower petals wither; at this stage the plants benefit from feeding with a liquid fertilizer every 10 to 12 days. You can pick the beans as soon as there is a sizeable crop of succulent young pods, and regular cropping will encourage the development of further pods.

# RUNNER BEANS

*This may seem an unusual choice for container growing – even indoors the plants grow very tall – but runner beans are rightly a gardeners' favorite. The taste and texture of freshly gathered young beans is unmatched by that of commercially grown produce.*

**R**unner bean plants in flower in the open garden are one of the most attractive sights of summer. In the indoor garden, they can certainly be counted among the most decorative of the vegetable plants, but you must be able to provide at least 6ft (1.8m) growing height to obtain a useful crop, and you will need to train the plants on long canes. The plants also need large containers, and for your own benefit the pots should not be grouped too closely – runner bean plants climb and cling to anything within range, and you could end up with an unmanageable tangle if they are allowed to intertwine with each other. If you see this happening, cut the crossing tendrils before they become inextricably engaged.

Despite this, runner beans are a highly worthwhile crop if you can provide the right conditions. They produce a generous crop for the space they occupy, and the beans are beautifully tender and well flavored if picked while still developing: they become coarser with age. In commercial growing, economics dictate mass harvests, which preclude selecting young beans at the perfect stage, so the quality of market vegetables can vary widely.

### Selecting runner beans for indoor growing
Few runner bean plants will crop as well indoors as they do in the open garden, so you should choose the most prolific varieties to obtain the maximum potential. Streamline is a cultivar producing slender pods up to 20in (50cm) long which I have found satisfactory for container growing. In the garden, Goliath is the perfect variety, highly productive with large, succulent pods, but allow for the fact that it will not do quite so well indoors. One with shorter pods – average 12in (30cm) in length – but an equally good cropper is Scarlet Emperor. All three bear attractive scarlet flowers.

Dwarf cultivars are available which can be grown in limited space,

---

**CULTIVATION CHECKLIST**

Sow two seeds to a 3in (8cm) pot at 2in (5cm) deep; allow to germinate in a moderate temperature

— • —

Discard weaker-growing seedlings, or separate seedlings into individual pots; transfer to 5in (13cm) pots as growth increases

— • —

Position containers in a sunny location; water frequently throughout the growing period

— • —

Provide 6ft (1.8m) canes on which the plants can climb

— • —

Feed weekly with liquid fertilizer as flower buds form

— • —

Spray with tepid water daily as flowers open to disperse pollen

— • —

Harvest the beans when they are of the required size

87

but the crop is naturally smaller in the size of the beans and the overall harvest. It is preferable to plant those of the larger varieties which can accustom themselves to containers.

## Sowing and germination

There are no special soil requirements for growing runner beans. A good soil-based potting medium is suitable, though you can add some peat or humus if preferred, and a little sand to improve drainage. Runner beans can be started in early spring indoors. Sow two seeds to a 3in (8cm) pot. Make hole in the soil 2in (5cm) deep and implant the seed upright, then fill the hole. The growing medium should be moist but not wet, and a moderate temperature is adequate – being basically garden varieties, these beans do not need excessive heat.

When the seedlings come up, remove the weaker of the two and allow the stronger one to grow on until it is time to transplant. If there seems little difference in quality, transfer one to a separate pot and grow on both plants. As they outgrow the small pots, pot them on into a one-size larger container. It is advisable to avoid root disturbance as much as possible, so the plants should only be transferred one more time after this, to the large pots or tubs in which they can mature and produce the crop.

Sow two runner beans to a pot and when the seedlings emerge, either remove the weaker-growing plant or separate the two and repot them individually.

## Training and support

Once the plants are in their final containers, support them with canes and as the plants increase in size, provide the 6ft (1.8m) canes on which they can climb freely. These can be inserted in the growing medium immediately at the same time that the plants are finally potted on, if the containers can be placed in their permanent site at this point. Water generously and make sure the water drains through the containers so there is no waterlogging of the soil. It is necessary to stand the pots or

**Indoor/outdoor growing**
Runner bean plants can be moved outdoors to a patio or balcony in late spring to early summer. Site them in a position where there is plenty of space for them to climb on long canes.

tubs in large trays to collect the excess water. Leaves wilt rapidly if the soil is insufficiently moist and in summer daily watering is required – twice daily in extremely hot weather.

When the plants have reached the top of the canes, pinch out the growing points. This has the effect of causing the plants to produce side shoots, and it is these which bear the flowers and subsequently the beanpods. Without pinching out, the plant will continue to produce leafy growth.

As soon as the flower buds form, start to water with diluted liquid fertilizer once a week. As the flowers open, spray with tepid water over several days to disperse pollen. A prolific plant produces flower buds over an extended period, so it is important to keep up the spraying to ensure that all the flowers are pollinated.

## Harvesting

Continue watering regularly as the beans develop – runner beans are thirsty plants and lack of moisture inhibits the crop. Start to pick beans as soon as they are of a good size for cooking. Check the plants every day and harvest in batches while the beans are still tender and smooth. If you leave them too long, the pods become coarse and stringy.

# ZUCCHINIS

*The zucchini, or courgette, is really an
immature vegetable marrow or squash. The
strains have been specially bred to provide a
small, tender vegetable with a variety of
culinary uses.*

**T**his is not just a smaller version of a larger vegetable, as development of zucchini cultivars has produced a sweeter taste and greater succulence than is obtained by harvesting very young vegetable marrows. Zucchinis make an attractive side vegetable when sliced and steamed or lightly fried, are good ingredients for a wide range of mixed vegetable and casserole dishes, can be added to salads and are delicious baked with a vegetable or meat filling.

This is a crop you can enjoy growing as much as you enjoy eating the produce. Zucchinis are not difficult to grow, though they do need regular attention.

### Selecting zucchinis for indoor growing

Most of the best cultivars available currently are of American origin and are listed in seed catalogues.

Aristocrat is a prolific all-female hybrid producing fruits with rich dark green skins. These are borne upright on the stems. Blondie, an F1 hybrid, has a light creamy tone to the green skins and the white flesh inside. It is an early-maturing type which crops heavily. Another F1 hybrid, Gold Rush, is a good choice and has attractive golden-yellow coloring. None of these hybrids requires pollination.

Burpee Golden Zucchini is a rich butter yellow, a dual-purpose plant which is equally tasty cooked or sliced thinly into a salad. It is also an excellent choice for container growing as it is compact and bushy in habit. Two types identified as 554 and 565 Zucchini provide a large harvest of tender, small fruits. These are varieties which do need to be pollinated to set fruit.

### Sowing and germination

A rich, fibrous potting medium is essential to successful growing of zucchinis. If you use a commercial soil-based mixture, add some peat to

---

**CULTIVATION CHECKLIST**

Sow seeds on edge, two to a 3in (8cm) pot; allow to germinate at minimum temperature 60°F (15°C)

— • —

Pot on into 5in (13cm) pots when seedlings have four true leaves

— • —

Stand pots on trays of pebbles and water moderately but frequently

— • —

Provide canes to support main stems as necessary

— • —

Feed weekly with liquid fertilizer through the flowering period; provide a humid atmosphere by spraying around the plants

— • —

Carry out hand-pollination as necessary

— • —

Harvest the zucchinis when they are young and tender

provide the fiber content. If you can make up your own growing medium, I recommend a mixture of one part loam, two parts peat and one part well-rotted horse manure for good results.

Sow the seed in early or mid spring, depending upon the conditions you can provide. To ensure germination, a minimum temperature of 60°F (15°C) must be maintained. Seeds are sown on edge, two to a 3in (8cm) pot, and covered with a ½in (1cm) layer of growing medium. Germination takes up to eight days.

## Growing on

As soon as the seedlings have developed four true leaves following the appearance of the cotyledons, they should be transplanted to larger pots. They can complete their development in 5in (13cm) pots, so only one repotting is necessary. This minimizes root disturbance.

Pot on zucchini seedlings only once, to avoid unnecessary damage to delicate roots.

Watering should be moderate but frequent. It is best to use a spray to moisten the compost gently and create humidity around the plants. Whatever your method, do not allow pools of water to form on the soil surface or around the base of the pot; this indicates that the compost is saturated, a poor condition for encouraging the growth of zucchinis. Stand the pots on trays of pebbles to allow water to drain freely.

As soon the plants begin to grow vigorously upwards, provide canes to support the main stems. Some varieties tend to straggle; these can be trimmed lightly to keep them within bounds but severe pruning is not advisable. Remove any uproductive laterals and large leaves which shade the flowering shoots.

When the plants are well established and just coming into flower, provide a weekly feed of liquid fertilizer diluted and watered into the soil. If you are not growing the all-female hybrids, the plants require pollination (see page 23) as the flowers open. Transfer the pollen from the male flowers of one plant to the female flowers of another. Self-

**Indoor/outdoor growing**
The plants can be moved outdoors in late spring when all danger of frost has passed. Attend to moisture and humidity requirements with regular watering and spraying.

pollination, that is, from male to female on the same plant, tends to produce fruits which are bitter to taste.

## Harvesting

The fruits swell rapidly after pollination and are usually ready to harvest within a few days if the plants are growing in a warm, sunny position. They are at their most sweet and tender in the early stages of ripening and lose these qualities if left on the plant too long. Continue to maintain humidity and watering of the soil during the harvesting period. Regular picking encourages fruiting and if you have several plants they may provide a continuous crop through the summer.

# EGGPLANTS

*Eggplant, or aubergine, is a fine plant to grow. It is beautiful, and its fruits have a high nutritional value. Long before the egg-shaped fruits appear, the plant produces gorgeous flowers, long-lasting and as attractive as any houseplant.*

The eggplant is usually among the more expensive of market vegetables, so if you have a taste for it, your own crop could represent a considerable saving. Essential ingredients for making ratatouille and moussaka, eggplants are also excellent as a side vegetable, plainly cooked or spiced, and make a useful addition to casserole dishes and stews.

The plants need careful cultivation, but are not difficult to grow indoors. They make a handsome feature, too, especially through the flowering period and during the ripening of the glossy purple-skinned fruits.

## Selecting eggplants for indoor growing

Black Prince is an all-female hybrid which can and does grow to 3ft (90cm) high. The special feature of this cultivar is that the fruits can be left on the plant for several weeks without becoming overripe or softened – a useful point if the harvesting time coincides with the holiday season. Another F1 hybrid, Black Enorma, produces fewer fruits, but each can weigh up to 1½lb (675g). Rather surprisingly, this plant is not so tall as Black Prince; 2ft (60cm) is the average height. But in both cases, the weight of the fruits is such that the plant will need supporting with canes and ties.

If you prefer smaller fruits, you can harvest them before they are fully grown (as long as they are mature enough for use), which encourages the plant to produce new fruits to replace them. Alternatively, you can select a hybrid called Short Tom, bearing fruits less than half the usual size. The plant itself is still quite large, growing to 2½ft (75cm). This variety is early flowering and prolific. There is an equivalent cultivar raised in the USA, called Modern Midget, which has the same qualities.

You might like to try the golden-yellow fruits of a variety commonly

**Staying in**
The eggplant is not suited to outdoor conditions and does not do well as a patio plant. It requires a warm, humid atmosphere which can best be provided indoors.

called the Oriental Eggplant. It grows to 2ft (60cm), and the golden fruits are more aptly described as egg-shaped than the longer produce of the other cultivars. They are also more strongly flavored than the purple fruits. The plant is not a female hybrid and requires hand-pollination.

## Sowing and germination

Eggplants have a somewhat longer growing season than other vege-tables – the period from sowing to harvest may be up to 20 weeks. If you can provide a daytime temperature of 72°F (22°C) and a minimum of 60°F (15°C) at night, you can sow the seed in early spring. The seeds cannot germinate at low temperatures and if subjected to cold and damp conditions will simply rot.

Sow one seed to a 3in (8cm) pot in a good peat-based potting mixture. The seeds take a little longer to germinate than most other vegetables, so it may be 14 days or more before you see them pushing through the surface. Nurture the seedlings in the same pots, watering regularly and spraying around the plants to maintain a humid atmosphere.

## Growing on

When the plants are 6in (15cm) high, they should be potted on into 8in (20cm) pots, in which they can complete their development. As they increase in size, encourage branching growth by pinching out the main growing point, so that the plant produces more lateral shoots which will bear the fruit. This should be done when the plant is about 8in (20cm) high.

Although eggplants thrive in the sun, they do not benefit from fierce midday heat beating through the window glass. While the sun is at its height, shield the plants with newspaper or draw the curtains. As soon

Eggplants are rather more delicate and have a longer growing season than other indoor-grown vegetables. Provide them with warm and humid conditions through all stages of growth.

## CULTIVATION CHECKLIST

Sow seeds singly in 3in (8cm) pots and allow to germinate at 72°F (22°C)

— · —

Keep potting mixture moist and maintain a humid atmosphere as seedlings develop

— · —

Transplant to 6in (15cm) pots when seedlings are 6in (15cm) high

— · —

Pinch out main growing points when plants are 8in high to encourage branching

— · —

Maintain regular watering and spraying; provide liquid feed every 10 days from the time when flower buds form

— · —

Support the main stem and fruit-bearing branches by tying them in to canes

— · —

Pollinate female flowers as they open, except in all-female hybrids

— · —

Harvest as ripening fruits achieve suitable size

as the hottest phase is past, allow the plants to stand in full light once again. Plenty of sunshine is essential for good development. Water daily in hot, dry conditions. If the leaves begin to wilt, you can revive them by watering generously, but it is far better to pay attention to their daily needs and not allow this situation to occur. Keep a humid atmosphere around the plants, as well as supplying moisture to the roots. Through the height of summer, spray the plants with tepid water every day. This has the advantage of at the same time discouraging red spider mite, the pest most likely to infest eggplants, although less likely to trouble plants grown indoors.

## Fruiting and harvest

As the flower buds appear, feed the plants with liquid fertilizer, adding it to the regular watering in the amount stated in the manufacturer's instructions. Provide the feed every ten days thereafter. By this time, each plant should have produced up to four fruit-bearing laterals, and fruits also form on the main stem and its branches. When the fruits develop, the plant is required to bear a considerable weight. To support stems and laterals, tie them to canes anchored firmly in the growing medium.

If you are not growing one of the female hybrids, the plant must be pollinated in order to set fruit. Use the hand-pollination method described on page 23 to transfer pollen from the male to the female flowers. You can then enjoy the sight of the fruit slowly forming and ripening. Harvest them when they are of a good size and firm to touch, but before the skins become dulled, which indicates that they are over-ripe and may taste bitter.

# MUSHROOMS

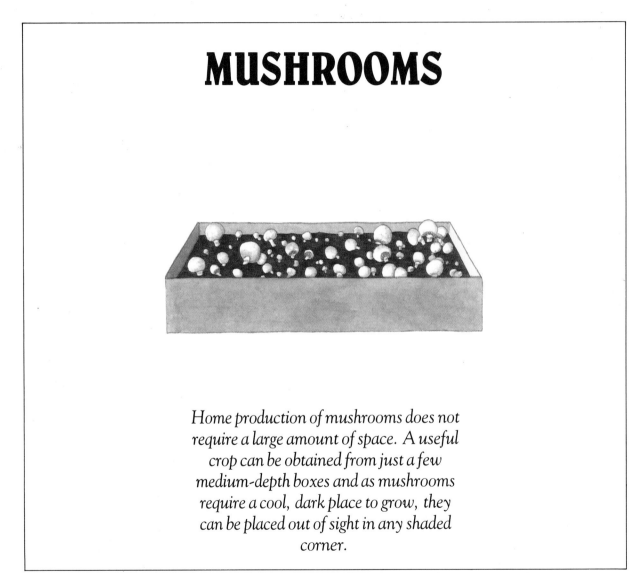

*Home production of mushrooms does not require a large amount of space. A useful crop can be obtained from just a few medium-depth boxes and as mushrooms require a cool, dark place to grow, they can be placed out of sight in any shaded corner.*

Gardening catalogues and some retail outlets offer complete mushroom-growing kits, but this is not the most economical way of going about things. There is an element of uncertainty about growing mushrooms, and the ready-spawned growing kits are often considered the most reliable method of producing a good crop. However, it is not a difficult process to prepare the containers and sow spawn; so if you accept the slight risk of disappointment it is worth while trying this vegetable, and there is the greater satisfaction when you succeed.

## Preparation

Mushroom spawn can be purchased separately and the growing mixture can be the same as that used for your other indoor crops. Horse manure is often recommended, and it is commonly thought that mushroom growing involves heaps of foul-smelling compost in which the mushrooms can thrive, but this is not the modern method. If you have access to horse manure it can be mixed with your usual potting medium. Provided the manure is well rotted it should be odorless, and you do not need large amounts. However, it is not essential.

A good growing medium is the spent mushroom compost from a previous cropping. This is occasionally offered for sale by the bag, or you may be able to acquire some from a mushroom-growing acquaintance. After raising your first crop, you will have your own spent compost. But as some of the nutrients have been used by the previous mushroom crop, do not use this as the sole growing medium; combine it with a commercial peat-based mixture.

Mushrooms are best grown in flat boxes or trays, as they do not need much depth, though plastic seed trays are a little too shallow. Wooden boxes of the type used by greengrocers and market traders for storing and transporting fruit and vegetables make ideal containers for mushrooms. These are often discarded when empty, or you may be able to buy them

### CULTIVATION CHECKLIST

Fill containers with growing medium; site in shade or darkness, or provide opaque covering to exclude light

— • —

Sprinkle mushroom spawn on the surface of the filled containers and cover with a fine layer of growing medium

— • —

Keep shaded and moist, at a temperature between 50°F (10°F) and 60°F (15°C)

— • —

Remove covering when mushrooms appear, about 3-4 weeks after sowing; do not move the containers to a lighter position

— • —

Harvest as the mushrooms reach the required size

99

quite cheaply from the trader. Plastic tubs also make good containers: you can use those sold for plant growing or recycle large containers of the type used to package ready-mixed adhesives and plasters. These should be thoroughly scrubbed with boiling water to remove all traces of their previous contents, which may have contained toxic chemicals. Add a little detergent to the washing water and give the tubs a final good rinse with clean water.

## Sowing and growing

Fill the containers to the top with the growing medium, moisten it lightly and firm it well. Sprinkle the mushroom spawn evenly over the surface and pat it in gently. Cover with the thinnest possible layer of the growing medium but do not firm this down as the pressure damages the spawn. It should be evenly moist, and in subsequent waterings it is best to use a very fine mist spray which will not disturb the delicate mycelium – the thread-like initial growths of the mushroom which are the equivalent of a root system.

A shaded location is essential. You can place the boxes in a cool, dark place such as under the kitchen sink or in a spare room or basement area. You can even put them under the bed, so in effect this is a space-saving crop, as the boxes do not take up valuable space on a sunny windowsill needed for your tomatoes and other more demanding plants. If you have no suitable hiding place, exclude the light by covering the containers with a few layers of newspaper or a sheet of black plastic. This should be loosely laid to allow ventilation; the mushrooms will develop mould if deprived of air, though a relatively damp atmosphere is not detrimental.

Apart from keeping the mushrooms shaded and moist, it is important to control the range of temperature. Extremes of heat and cold will cause the crop to fail. An average between 50°F (10°C) and 60°F (15°C)

**Staying in**
Mushrooms must be grown undisturbed in a cool, dark location and are not suited to outdoor cultivation.

is most suitable, and the temperature should not rise above the upper limit. The spawn may be killed by temperatures much higher than this, so this aspect of cultivation needs particular attention during the warmer months of the year. Likewise winter crops need protection; the environment should be cool, but not cold.

Assuming all the conditions are favorable, the mushrooms should start to push up above the surface within about four weeks of sowing. Check on their progress after about three weeks and remove any covering as soon as you see the tiny white 'buttons' appear on the surface of the growing medium. Once this has occurred, uncover the containers but do not expose them to bright light. Fungi are plants of the shade, unlike green plants which need the sunlight in order to produce chlorophyll.

## Harvesting

If you remove some mushrooms at the 'button' stage, those which remain have more space in which to grow and can become larger. (The tiny buttons, sliced very thinly, are delicious raw in salads.) To take out a mushroom, twist it carefully – do not pull it sharply upwards or you will dislodge the mycelium of other mushrooms not yet grown. If any pieces are left behind from the mushrooms you have removed, be sure to take them out also; if left in the growing medium they will quickly rot and may spoil the remainder of the crop.

About one pound (450g) of mushrooms is produced in a square foot (900cm$^2$) of growing area. If you have plenty of space and would like to grow mushrooms in quantity to obtain a continuous supply (they can be sown at any time of year), obtain a number of containers and stack them in a staggered arrangement as they are filled. As you harvest one crop, simply rearrange the containers and reuse those which have been emptied to house the next sowing.

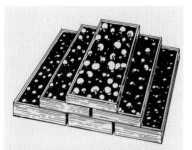

Accommodate a large crop of mushrooms by stacking the boxes in tiers. Open out the arrangement as the mushrooms develop so the upper boxes do not restrict the growth of the mushrooms in the tray beneath.

# SPINACH

*Continuous sowings from early spring through summer and autumn provide fresh spinach crops for most of the year – for salads, vegetarian dishes and as a side vegetable that can be spiced up or dressed down.*

Spinach is often considered to be an acquired taste. Although some find it rather boring as a side vegetable, there are various ways to serve it – such as tossed in butter or simmered in spices – which bring out the best of this vigorous leaf crop. It is delicious in mixed vegetable dishes, in quiche and with hot cheese, and makes a tasty soup. The young leaves are also much appreciated as a green salad item. It has a reputation for being a particularly nutritious vegetable, but is equally to be valued as a versatile cooking ingredient.

## Selecting spinach for indoor growing

Spinach is categorized in two types: summer, or round-seeded varieties, and winter, or prickly-seeded spinach. For indoor growing, it is not necessary to divide these types too strictly, as one or two of these cultivars can be grown at any time.

Longstanding Round is a round-seeded variety recommended for early sowing. Symphony is a large-leaved F1 hybrid which is also early-cropping. Sigmaleaf is a useful variety which may be harvested over a longer period and does not run rapidly to seed. This can also be grown as a winter variety.

Of the winter types, Broad-leaved Prickly is a standard variety for sowing in late summer to early autumn. Another good large-leaved prickly-seeded type which is said to resist bolting is Greenmarket; this can also be grown as a summer crop.

There is a third type of spinach known as New Zealand variety, which is actually a dwarf beet grown only for its mild-flavored foliage. It is also described as perpetual spinach, or spinach beet.

## Sowing and germination

Grow both summer and winter varieties in small batches, sown successionally, so that you have a series of manageable crops which can be

---

### CULTIVATION CHECKLIST

Sow seed in trays at 1in (2.5cm) apart, or in individual pots. Allow to germinate at 50-60°F (10-15°C)

— · —

Transfer young plants to larger containers at 4-6in (10-15cm) apart; provide humus-rich growing medium

— · —

Site plants in a bright but not sunny position and keep well watered

— · —

Harvest young leaves for use in salads; allow to grow on for use as a cooked vegetable used before the plants run to seed. For summer cropping, start sowings from early spring. Spinach needs a rich, deep soil; add some humus to proprietary brand potting mixture and allow a generous container size when the plants are potted on.

Sow seeds in trays spaced at 1in (4cm) apart and ½-1in (1-2.5cm) deep, or sow in individual pots. If you cannot easily separate the seeds while sowing, wait until the seedlings appear and thin out the weakest growth.

When sowing New Zealand spinach, soak the seeds in water overnight beforehand and sow them to a depth of 1in (2.5cm) in the soil. This is best grown for a single harvest, rather than by successional sowings.

## Growing on

When the young plants are large enough to handle, transfer them to larger containers. Space them at 3-4in (8-10cm) apart if you intend to harvest young leaves for salad use. If you are growing on the leaves for use as a cooked vegetable, 6in (15cm) apart is adequate. If growing the spinach plants in individual pots, make sure these provide a good depth of soil.

Keep the plants well watered and provide a light location, but shield them from direct sun, as this causes spinach to run to seed. Pinch out the growing tips of New Zealand variety as the young plants develop to maintain compact growth.

Harvesting can begin about eight weeks after sowing if you are taking young salad leaves. In some varieties, it may take a few more weeks to produce a useful crop. Do not remove more than half the leaves of a summer variety at one time, and take fewer from the winter types. Selective culling encourages further production. Harvest spinach beet by taking a few leaves from the base of each plant at every picking.

**Indoor/outdoor growing**
Indoor-sown plants can be moved outdoors when all frosts have passed. Sowings can be made in containers sited outside from late spring onwards.

# INDOOR TO OUTDOOR CROPS

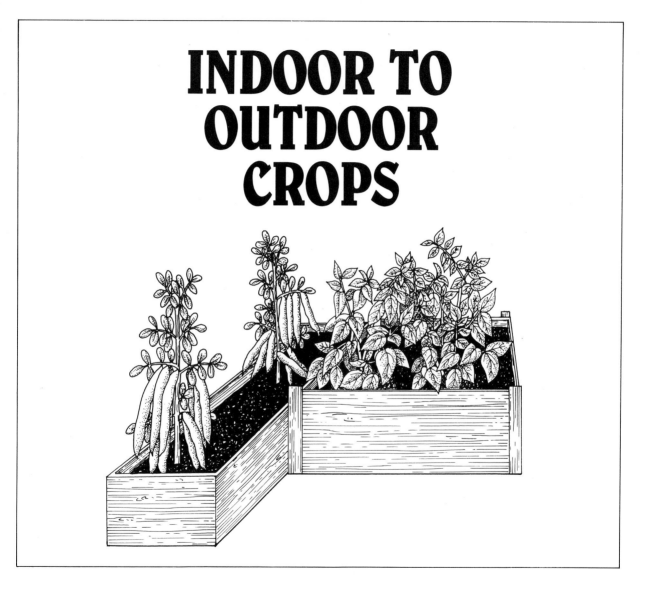

# POTATOES

*Potatoes may not seem like natural
candidates for container growing, but you
can harvest delicious early new potatoes
from your patio if you have space for a few
large pots or boxes.*

**A**s long as potatoes remain a staple food they will be an attractive prospect to gardeners, and though you may not be able to harvest a bumper crop from containers, you can certainly enjoy the finest quality. Potatoes are categorized under first early, second early and maincrop grades, and though the choices are restricted for container growing, there are a few varieties of first earlies which produce good results. The second early and maincrop potatoes are best suited to growing in open ground – you would have to give a considerable amount of space to maincrops and it is hardly worth it as they are among the least expensive of market vegetables.

Even for the smaller new potatoes, you need to have space for a group of large pots – the minimum practical size is 12in (30cm) deep and 8in (20cm) across. Large wooden boxes make ideal containers for potatoes. You may be able to find crates used for storing and transporting vegetable produce; if they are solid at the base, remember to punch holes in them to allow drainage. It is because this crop needs a relatively large area for growing that it is best to site the containers on a patio or balcony out of the way of domestic traffic, but potatoes can be grown indoors if that is your only option.

## Selecting potatoes for container growing

Potatoes are not grown from seed but from seed potatoes, tubers which have been specially selected, bred and grown to produce plants capable of developing crops of edible tubers. You cannot use ordinary potatoes which have begun to sprout; these produce at best a poor-quality, slow-growing, limited crop. Seed potatoes can be obtained from markets, garden centers and specialist growers and are usually sold by weight. Make sure that they are certified disease-free and conforming to standard growing regulations.

The varieties which I can most strongly recommend for container

---

**CULTIVATION CHECKLIST**

Place seed potatoes to sprout in a box exposed to light, in cool or moderate temperatures

— • —

Plant sprouted tubers in pots 12in (30cm) deep and 8in (20cm) or more across; or plant at least 8in (20cm) apart in a deep wooden box

— • —

Water moderately; increase watering in hot, dry conditions

— • —

Draw up soil around the base of the plant to exclude light completely from the developing potatoes

— • —

Harvest when flowers on the plants have faded and the leaves begin to turn yellow growing are Arran Pilot and Pentland Javelin. These both have white flesh; Arran Pilot is a kidney-shaped potato while Pentland Javelin is oval. Home Guard and Foremost are good choices, both white-fleshed and oval.

### Sprouting tubers and planting

The seed potatoes are not planted straight into soil; they have first to be sprouted, that is, allowed to produce shoots from the potato 'eyes'. Lay them in a shallow box and leave them exposed to the light – they do not need a covering. Position each tuber with some of the eyes uppermost, to allow them to sprout freely. I do not recommend cutting seed potatoes into pieces unless they are very large, which is unlikely with these varieties; a cut surface increases susceptibility to rotting.

The tubers require only a cool or moderate temperature while sprouting, but must not be exposed to frost. The sprouts should be sufficiently developed for the seed potatoes to be planted within four to five weeks. Check their development periodically; if they are spindly and pale, they are not getting enough light. Ideally, the shoots should be short and stout.

Regular planting time for potatoes is early to mid spring; container-grown crops can have a head start, but do not plant them outdoors if frosts are still likely. Fill the containers with soil-based growing mixture, preferably with some added silver sand, leaf mould or peat, or a little of each. Horse manure is a good addition if you can obtain it, and a handful of bonemeal is beneficial. It is best to plant up the containers in situ, as they will be heavy once filled with soil.

Plant the tubers with the sprouted eyes uppermost. Cover them with soil to about 4in (10cm) deep and firm the surface. Water the containers moderately; the soil must not be allowed to become saturated, as waterlogging rots potatoes very quickly.

Seed potatoes are packed into an open box with the potato eyes exposed to light to encourage sprouting. When they have developed sturdy shoots they can be planted up in containers.

As the plants mature, draw up the soil around the base of each plant to exclude all light from reaching the developing tubers.

## Growing on

A potato crop thrives best in moderate temperatures. Outdoor conditions during spring should suit the plants quite well, unless there is an unexpected cold snap. Maintain moderate watering through all stages of growth, increasing the water supply only on very hot days in the summer months. The top growth of the potato plants may be self-supporting, but if the stems tend to lean or fall, support them by tying them to canes.

You may be aware of the process of 'earthing-up' garden-grown potatoes. This simply means drawing up soil around the base of the plant to prevent light from reaching the newly formed tubers. If the potatoes are exposed to light they become green and are inedible – a green potato is poisonous – and should this happen, do not attempt to use the potatoes in cooking. Adapt the earthing-up process to your containers, drawing up soil from the sides of the pot towards the base of the plant, or adding a little more growing medium if necessary.

## Harvesting

Potato plants eventually come into flower, and the time to harvest is after the flowers have faded and the foliage has begun to turn yellow. Small new potatoes taste particularly delicious, but if you prefer to let them increase in size, simply leave the plant in the container a little longer. When the leaves have lost all green coloring, however, the potatoes cease to grow, as the plant is no longer manufacturing food for the tubers by the process of photosynthesis.

# PEAS

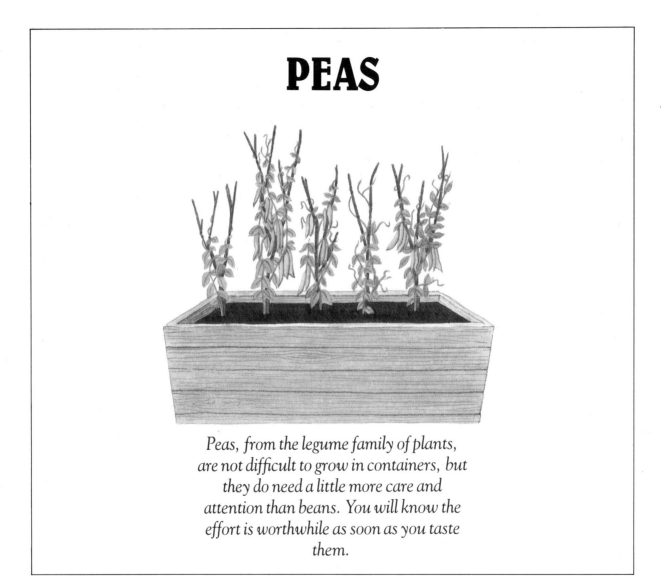

*Peas, from the legume family of plants, are not difficult to grow in containers, but they do need a little more care and attention than beans. You will know the effort is worthwhile as soon as you taste them.*

**T** fresh peas are in a different league for flavor and texture, especially
fresh peas are in a different league for flavour and texture, especially
if you harvest them young and cook them lightly within minutes of
picking. Home-grown peas even surpass the quality of the fresh varieties
sold in their pods in season, as the peas begin to lose their sweetness
soon after the pods are taken from the plant.

## Selecting peas for container growing

Peas can be categorized as wrinkle-seeded, round-seeded and edible-
podded varieties. The wrinkle-seeded cultivars are sweeter in flavor
and more succulent than the round-seeded kinds, but until recent
horticultural improvements were much later in cropping. This situation
was changed by the introduction of the cultivar known as Hurst Beagle,
a wrinkle-seeded pea which can compete with any early round-seeded
variety on the market. It has another great advantage for the container-
gardener; it is a tiny dwarf cultivar with pods averaging 3-3½in (8-9cm)
in length: there are six to eight peas in each pod. Although this plant
grows to 18in (45cm) in height in the open garden, it rarely reaches
more than 12in (30cm) when container-grown, but still produces a
profusion of pods.

Other wrinkle-seeded peas include the redoubtable Kelvedon
Wonder, which I have grown both in the garden and in containers, and
found little difference in cropping potential. It grows to 18in (45cm) in
height and needs supporting. The small pods – about 3in (8cm) in
length – are profuse and their sharply pointed ends make for easy
podding when you are preparing the peas for cooking. This cultivar is a
very good choice for succession sowing; by putting in seeds every two
weeks until midsummer, you can have crops right through late autumn.

Another useful wrinkle-seeded pea is Little Marvel, which grows to
15in (38cm) and is a prolific podder. The peas are exquisitely sweet, and

---

### CULTIVATION CHECKLIST

Sow seed in early spring, in trays or
singly in 3in (8cm) pots

— • —

Provide a light, warm location as
seedlings appear

— • —

Pot on into containers 8in (20cm)
or more deep as growth increases;
move plants outdoors when danger
of frosts is passed

— • —

Water generously but avoid
waterlogging of the soil

— • —

Support plants on bushy pea sticks
or strong, slender twiggy branches

— • —

Provide netting as protection from
birds

— • —

Feed every ten days with liquid
fertilizer from the time when flower
buds develop

— • —

Harvest when the young pods are
succulent and easy to open

if you like raw or lightly cooked peas for inclusion in salad, this is the one to choose. Like the preceding variety, it is also a good choice for succession sowing. The variety known as Winfrida, which grows to a height of about 15in (38cm), can be sown throughout autumn, indoors or out, or from late winter to early spring to get ahead on the growing season. In mild areas, it can be started in containers outdoors; trials have proved it capable of withstanding light frost and it is the hardiest cultivar of all.

Among the round-seeded peas, I can recommend Feltham First Early as a good choice for container growing. Meteor is a more compact plant, but needs good root space and should be potted up in a large pot size. Round-seeded peas are generally larger than the wrinkle-seeded types, both as plants and in the size of the pods, and require firm support from pea sticks or canes as they grow. On account of this, I consider round-seeded peas less suitable for container growing than the wrinkle-seeded types described above, but it is worth studying the qualities of other proven garden cultivars if you have reasonable space for your pea crop and are prepared for an element of experiment in growing them in containers.

The edible-podded peas, also called sugar peas or mangetout, are unfortunately not really suited to the limited space of container growing. The majority of the cultivars grow up to 6ft (1.8m) tall; even those described as dwarf varieties are 2ft (60cm) high or more. They need considerable lateral space in which to grow, as well as height, and larger containers with correspondingly more soil. Many are rather slow to mature, and more suitable for greenhouse cultivation. My own opinion is that they do not provide a good return for the time and trouble spent on them, and since your area for cultivation is restricted, it is better to keep to the vegetables that have proven success in container growing.

**Staying in**
Plants can be maintained indoors throughout the flowering period to harvesting the peapods if a sunny, well-ventilated position is provided.

## Sowing and growing

When you have selected the cultivar you wish to grow, prepare the containers with the growing medium. Peas are not particular about soil type; they thrive in most conditions, but the better the soil mixture, the better the crop. The seeds can be sown in seed trays or boxes, or if preferred you can start them off singly, one seed to a 3in (8cm) pot. The advantage of this method is that you can use plastic propagator tops, or improvised equivalent (see page 14) to give them extra protection while germination and early growth occurs. This is especially necessary if you start the seeds out of doors. Low temperatures inhibit germination, however, so the location in which the seeds are allowed to germinate depends upon the time of sowing and conditions indoors and out.

Spring sowing is the rule for garden-grown crops, but for peas started indoors you gain an extended growing season as with other vegetables. Early sowings can be started from late winter or, as explained, in the autumn preceding the growing season. Practise succession sowing if you can provide the space for a large pea crop, starting a new batch about every 14 days. Remember, however, that accommodating germinating seeds is one thing; finding space for large pots, troughs or tubs when the plants are grown is a different matter.

Do not flatten the soil too firmly after sowing the seed; a light, crumbly texture is ideal. Germination takes about seven to ten days. As the seedlings appear, provide a position in good light and with a warm, but not hot atmosphere. If you have sown into small pots, transfer growing plants into larger containers as necessary. Allow about 8in (20cm) of soil depth for the maturing plants, as well as lateral space for the growth to spread. Water freely, but note that although thirsty plants, peas do not like waterlogging. When the plants are well established, the containers can be moved outside onto the patio or balcony once the danger of night frosts has passed.

Pea plants need to climb and spread, firmly supported on twiggy sticks.

## Support and protection

As the plants grow, they need supporting. The very dwarf varieties do not always require this, but the larger plants do better and produce more pods if they have upright sticks on which to climb. You can use the traditional bushy pea sticks, or insert in the soil some twiggy stems or branches from a tree or shrub; select branches which are slender but have reasonable strength. When pushing the supporting sticks into the tub or trough, take care to avoid cutting through the plants' root systems: if you encounter resistance, insert the stick elsewhere until you find a point where it slides easily into the soil. Tie in stems and growing shoots to anchor the plants to the supports.

Plants grown outdoors are vulnerable to birds, which enjoy the tender young growth. The system of criss-cross threads tied to sticks, which works very well to deter birds in the open garden, is not very practical for containers. The most effective way of protecting your plants is to erect netting 'cages', making a frame of wooden laths to support the nets. If you have quite a large crop you can use wire netting to add strength to the structure, attached to the laths with wire staples. Plastic netting can be substituted, however, and this may be found more manageable and easily obtainable.

## Harvesting

The plants should be regularly fed with a liquid fertilizer as soon as the flower buds appear. One feed every ten days is quite sufficient as the flowers fade and the pods develop. Keep up regular watering, and do not allow the growing medium either to dry out or to become saturated.

The peas are ready for harvest when the young pods are springy and tender, opening easily with a snapping noise when you press the pointed end with your finger. If the pods are drum-tight and opened with difficulty, the peas will be past their best.

# BROAD BEANS

*This is an excellent crop for patio growing, providing succulent pods in the young stage and large, tasty beans when developed. Broad beans, also called fava beans, provide a generous summer harvest.*

**B**road beans, or fava beans, can be eaten in two ways, both delicious. If the pods are harvested very young, they can be sliced and cooked like runner beans. In the later stages, the beans are extracted from the pods, which are discarded, and cooked separately. Either way they are particularly good served tossed in butter or with a white sauce.

This is one crop for which you do need outdoor growing space – I have had excellent results when the beans have been started outdoors and allowed to develop in the open, but you can germinate the seed in indoor conditions and put the young plants outdoors after potting on. They adapt well to container growing, though perhaps yielding a smaller crop than would be the case in open ground.

## Selecting broad beans for indoor growing

Aquadulce is an early-cropping longpod variety which can be started in late autumn or late winter to produce the first harvest of the following growing season. The bean pods can grow to 15in (38cm) long. A good choice for spring sowing is Bunyard's Exhibition, with pods growing 12-14in (30-35cm) in length. Imperial Green Longpod is the giant, with pods up to 20in (50cm), but take into account that the longpod varieties are large plants needing wide, deep containers.

Windsor cultivars are smaller plants very well suited to container growing. Bonnie Lad forms compact, erect plants about 12in (30cm) high providing pods 5-6in (13-15cm). The beanpods are generously clustered and extremely tasty when sliced and cooked. Another useful small plant is The Sutton, which is the same height as Bonnie Lad, but the pods are slightly smaller at 4-5in (10-13cm).

## Sowing and germination

Broad beans like a rich, well-composted soil which holds moisture; they do not produce a good crop in poor soil mixtures. It is best to make up a

---

### CULTIVATION CHECKLIST

Sow singly in 3in (8cm) pots at 2in (5cm) deep; allow to germinate in moderate temperatures indoors or out

— • —

Pot on into 7in (17cm) pots as growth develops, or plant in tubs or troughs at 6-8in (15-20cm) apart; move indoor-sown plants outdoors

— • —

Water freely throughout the plants' development

— • —

Harvest the beanpods when young and tender to use the whole pod; leave until the beans grow larger if these are to be removed from the pod for cooking

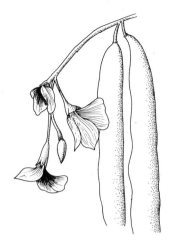

suitable growing mixture from three parts soil-based potting mixture, one part silver sand and one part humus. If you have garden soil available, use this as one part of the growing medium and reduce the amount of potting mixture. The humus you can obtain bagged from a garden supplier, or you can crumble in dried leaves (see page 17).

The beans should be sown singly with 3in (8cm) of growing space if you intend to pot them on, 6in (15m) for dwarf varieties or 8in (20cm) for the larger kinds if you are sowing direct into the containers in which they will grow and crop. Insert the seed 2in (5cm) deep in the soil, fill the planting hole and firm the soil surface. It is best to sow into moist soil and you can spray lightly after sowing if it seems insufficiently moist.

Broad beans are resilient and can be placed outside on a windowsill, patio or balcony to germinate. Alternatively, keep them in a fairly cool place indoors. Growth should appear above the soil between seven and fourteen days after sowing.

## Growing on

This is one of the easiest of crops for cultivation. Broad beans need very little attention except to be kept well watered. If the growing medium is nutritious, no feeding is required. Early sowings should produce plants in flower by late spring to early summer. You can harvest the beans between three and four months after sowing in spring. Autumn-sown crops can be expected to be ready at about the same time, as the growing cycle is longer because of the slow period of winter growth.

**Indoor/outdoor sowing**
Broad beans do best outdoors, so indoor-sown plants should be moved to a patio or balcony once established in their final containers. The beans can also be sown directly into containers sited outdoors in a reasonably sheltered spot.

| Vegetable | Sowing/starting time | Germination time | Temperature for germination | Sowing to harvest | Light requirements |
|---|---|---|---|---|---|
| **Broad beans** | Late autumn or early spring | 5-10 days | 55-60°F (13-15°C) | about 14 weeks | Good light |
| **Chilli peppers** | Mid spring | 20-30 days | 75°F (24°C) | 4-5 months | Sun |
| **Cucumbers** | Late spring | 6-9 days | 75°F (24°C) min 60°F (15°C) | 8-16 weeks (F1 hybrids earlier) | Sun |
| **Eggplants** | Early to mid spring | 14 days or more | 72°F (22°C) | 4-5 months | Sun |
| **French beans** | Early to mid spring | 5-10 days | min 50°F (10°C) | 12-14 weeks | Good light |
| **Green onions** | Early spring onwards | 12-20 days | min 55°F (13°C) | 6-8 weeks | Average light |
| **Land cress** | Early spring onwards | 8-12 days | 50-60°F (10-15°C) | 8 weeks | Good light |
| **Lettuces** | Early spring | 4-10 days | min 50°F (10°C) | 8-12 weeks | Bright, protected from hot sun |
| **Melons** | Late spring | 20-25 days | 75°F (24°C) | 20-22 weeks (from germination) | Sun |
| **Mushrooms** | At any time | 4 weeks | max 60°F (15°C) | 4 weeks | Shade |
| **Peas** | Autumn or spring | 9-10 days | min 50°F (10°C) | 12-14 weeks | Average light |
| **Potatoes** | Early spring | 4-5 weeks | 60°F (15°C) | 4 months | Average light |
| **Radishes** | At any time | 5-7 days | min 50°F (10°C) | 25 days | Bright, no direct sun |
| **Runner beans** | Early spring | 12-18 days | min 55°F (13°C) | 12-14 weeks | Average light |
| **Spinach** | Early spring onwards | 5-10 days | 60°F (15°C) | 8-12 weeks | Good light |
| **Sprouting beans and grains** | At any time | 3-5 days | min 55°F (13°C) | 3-6 days | Shade or darkness |
| **Sweet peppers** | Mid spring | 20-30 days | 75°F (24°C) | 4-5 months | Sun |
| **Tomatoes** | Mid spring to mid summer | 9 days | 60-65°F (15-18°C) | 52 days average | Sun |
| **Zucchinis** | Early to mid spring | 14-21 days | min 60°F (15°C) | 3½-5 months | Sun |

# INDEX

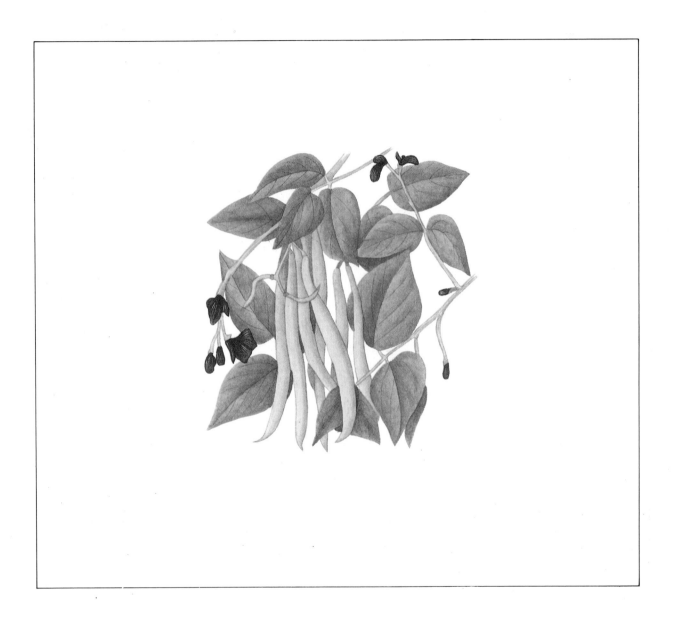